# REMARKABLE
# SERVICE

## How to Keep
## Your Doors Open

Mike Mack, MBA

D1042496

REMARKABLE SERVICE – "How to Keep Your Doors Open"

Printed by:
CreateSpace Independent Publishing Platform

Published in the United States of America

151019-00259.3

ISBN-13: 978-1978413252
ISBN-10: 1978413254

# Dedication to Vernon Hibbard

When I was in my early teens I had the good fortune to work for and learn from one of the most successful business owners I knew at that time. Vernon Hibbard taught me so much about life and business from 1976 until 2016. He passed away in January 2017 at the age of 91. I dedicate this revised edition of my book to my first mentor and lifelong friend, Vernon.

In August 2010, I wrote a blog titled **"Life Lessons.....from Wisdom!"** after interviewing Vernon and I would like to share it with all of you.

Vernon has been a long-time family friend, former boss and life mentor to me. I have known Vernon my entire life! He is 85 years young and I regard him as one of the brightest business minds that I know. We always enjoy meaningful discussion on the phone or whenever we are together. I always find time in my schedule when travelling to Saskatchewan to see him because I always learn something. (I also apply my long-time guiding principle here as well. **"I am glad I did visit him vs. I wish I had."**)

I asked Vernon what he regarded as his Life Lessons in the past 85 years.

Here are some of Vernon's thoughts:

He said *"Mike, you are like me..., your ears are eager to hear and learn."*

I guess it is true, because I love listening to absolutely anything Vernon has to say, regardless of topic.

When he was in his early teens and his parents would visit the neighbours on the farm, he would sit with the adults rather than play with the kids his age, as he wanted to learn something. Vernon said, *"You should always learn as you go."*

When he started his Farm Equipment dealership in 1949, (Hibbard Equipment) he earned solid customers and they trusted him and he in turn trusted them. They had confidence in him as a businessman.

Vernon noted that *"Today, the world is changing so fast, you need to keep up! Are you keeping up Mike?"*

He's a man who has always had a passion for learning, seeing the world and he loves to travel.

Vernon stated, *"Nature is becoming more of my enjoyment, it is great to see Mother Nature at work."* That would explain his passion for farming and for travel.

He has a lot less focus on business today. Seeing his grand kids and now his great grand kids grow-up, has become very important to him. "*They are true enjoyment!*" He noted that the difference with your kids and your grandkids is that you tell your kids to "slow down" and now you get to watch the grand kids run!

Back in 2009 over dinner, Vernon and I shared some deep dialogue about life and he commented about the changes we experience in life. He said, "*Mike, nothing lasts forever, we change, and people change and go in different directions, just accept it.*" This was extremely valuable advice for me at the time!

I asked Vernon what he would like to be remembered for? He laughed, and said, "*I am not sure I should be remembered for anything, other than the fact that I am no different than anyone else. I looked after myself, and loved what I did in business and loved my family and tried to enjoy life.*" I know for certain that he truly loved what he did from a business perspective. He said "*If I had to do it all over again, I would.*"

I am grateful that Vernon took the time to share this wisdom with me, but I am truly honoured that I had him as a dear friend and life mentor.

Vernon was like a father to me and I was blessed to know him my entire life. While I am sad that Vernon is no longer with us, I am extremely grateful that I learned so much from him over all these years and that our friendship continued and lasted all this time. **Rest in peace Vernon!**

# Here's What's Inside...

*"We keep moving forward, opening new doors, and doing new things, because we're curious and curiosity keeps leading us down new paths."*

-Walt Disney

# Introduction

It is my belief that Remarkable Customer Service can improve revenue and overall corporate profitability. It can open doors for your business and if you do a poor job of taking care of your customers, you may find your doors closed! Every business has the ability to create and deliver Remarkable Service. Do you believe this?

The Revised and Expanded Edition of this book is packed with unforgettable Customer Service stories. Some are truly Remarkable in a great way and some are so bad that we will remark about the story and the businesses involved for a very long time.

I offer my sincere thanks to all of the amazing people who took the time to contribute their Remarkable stories to this book. From India, New York, San Francisco, Las Vegas, Halifax, Toronto, Edmonton, Vancouver, Germany, and more.

Learn what it takes to ensure that your doors stay open, regardless of economic conditions.

What is Remarkable Service and is it sustainable?

Why do some organizations give it and why do some consistently screw up?

Learn what it takes to deliver Remarkable Service and why everyone on your team has to understand that the "little things" make all the difference.

When I was a teenager, I lived and worked in a small town: Minton, Saskatchewan, Canada. I learned at a very young age the importance of providing great customer service at my first job as a Parts Department Assistant at a small farm equipment dealership called Hibbard Equipment. (My earliest mentor, the late Vernon Hibbard was the founder of this business and I dedicated this book to him, as he taught me so much about life, business and how to treat customers.)

Most of our customers were farmers living in Canada as well as the U.S.A., as we were close to the Montana border. Many customers were demanding because they needed service and parts to repair broken-down farm equipment that was vital to their livelihoods. Time was often of the essence so that they could do their farming when the weather was favourable. In fact, it wasn't uncommon for them to call me at 11:00 at night or 5:00 in the morning, requesting that I go down to the "shop" so they could purchase a part to repair their broken equipment. I always regarded it as my "duty and obligation" because I was paid to deliver good customer service. (I didn't know at the time whether it was Remarkable or not, but I did know that it was important!) As I became more experienced, I got to know many customers and it was evident that most of them genuinely appreciated the support and service. While it was on a small scale, customer service became ingrained in my DNA and has remained that way throughout my career. I learned that when you treat customers well and show them respect, they usually come back. What a concept!!!

The reality is that we all appreciate being treated well as a customer. Perhaps the cashier at the local grocery store waves you ahead in the line; your car is a little extra shiny after you pick it up from a service; the restaurant server gives you a piece of cheesecake on the house; all because they appreciate you as a customer. We want it, we hope for it, and for the most part, we expect it.

After becoming an entrepreneur and starting my own business in 2006, I knew that customer service was a vital component of retaining customers. Keeping our customers happy may eventually earn us the right to ask for a referral or gain more business. In the early years of my business, I put a greater focus of my energy into improving sales for our customers (i.e. sales coaching, training and consulting). While customer service was important, more customers looked to us to support them with improving their sales - growth in sales, putting more sales in the pipeline, a higher volume of new customers for their businesses, etc. While this was valuable for my customers, I found there was much more to offer them as part of my service offering. Sales and Service must always go hand in hand. You may be able to close a sale, but if you don't deliver reliable and consistent service to your customer, you can't expect to earn another sale from that customer. Regardless of how well the economy is doing or what the price of oil is at any given time, Customer Service is the one thing that any business can control and improve upon 24/7, 365 days a year. But it's all about progress, not perfection. You can't fix everything in your business in one fell swoop. It takes time and patience, requiring constant and never-ending improvement.

In my opinion, many businesses don't put enough focus, attention and effort into their customer service. They don't hire the right people, or train their employees. Owners or managers may not be aligned and act dysfunctional, creating departmental silos that don't serve the best interest of their customer. I want to bring more awareness to businesses so that they can make their customer service experiences better and ideally, remarkable, regardless of their industry. I also want businesses to feel great about it in the process. While I can think of several examples of truly Remarkable Service, unfortunately I can think of many more examples that aren't so good. Ultimately as customers, we expect more and we deserve more and YOUR customers think the same way.

I hope this book creates greater awareness of the value of creating Remarkable Customer Service, offers suggestions to improve your business service levels, and encourages you to find creative ways to keep your doors open.

Enjoy the revised edition of my book!

Here's to keeping your doors open!

*Mike*

# Can Your Business Be Remarkable?

Regardless of
your business
or industry
you can create
*Remarkable Service*

Any business in any industry can be Remarkable!

Here's how:

While the word "remarkable" is not new, it aligns well with my belief that customer service can be Remarkable. But what does remarkable mean exactly? Does your business do something that your customers would "remark" about? It doesn't have to be big, but it should be memorable and impactful enough to your customer so that they will remark about it to others or they may even share it with a lot of people. That could be a great story or a brutal example of extremely poor service. I will share many of both in the coming pages.

Remarkable can be simple and it doesn't have to cost your business a lot of money, but it can make your business more money, through enhanced revenues, sales and overall corporate profitability. I want everyone who reads this book to look at their business with a different lens and think like a customer. I want to create awareness that service challenges may exist in your business and encourage you to do something about it, to think like your customers, and perhaps see that your customer service delivery and approach could be much better.

Here's a view from a customer perspective, with several industry examples:

### Restaurant

You listen to your customers concerns and do your very best to accommodate their request. Whether the steak is not the way you like, or the music is too loud, fix it and smile while doing it. This can bring your customer back again and again. You may say this is Remarkable.

### Health Care

You have a team of Hearing Aid Practitioners, and many of your customers/patients are seniors. A few of them have trouble visiting your office. A team member drives to the patient's house for a hearing test. They stay after the appointment for tea and learn more about the senior patient's family. Some say this is Remarkable Service.

## Owner/Entrepreneur

You operate a photography studio. One of your customer's children is getting married and the customer invites you to the wedding. You offer to shoot complimentary wedding photos, as you will be at the wedding anyway. This saves the young couple thousands of dollars. Many would say this is Remarkable.

## Farm Equipment Dealership

You may have late hours of operation and 24-hour service for your farming customers during seeding and harvest. If a customer needed a part at 5:00 a.m. and your team took the call and served the customer, many would say that is Remarkable Service.

## Legal/Accounting/Financial Services

One of your customers may have an important tax question about their business. They call you and catch you on the eighth hole of a golf course in mid-summer, but you take the call (Thanks Quentin!). Some would say that is Remarkable Service.

## Engineering/Construction

A developer has a big issue with zoning and they have a deadline to reach in order to get construction underway. Your team works through the weekend to tweak vital details so that they are prepared. Many would say that is Remarkable Service.

## Call Centre

A young lady calls in about the need to return a pair of shoes that her mother purchased. Your call centre representative discovers that the young lady's mother passed away recently and there is no receipt for the shoes. You offer a full refund and send a money order to the young lady. When the money arrives via courier, a beautiful bouquet of flowers and a sympathy card is attached. Many would say that is Remarkable and the young lady tells hundreds of people about this Remarkable experience.

## Heavy-Duty Truck Dealership

Your business has a customer that operates several trucks in their fleet and their shop is two hours from your shop. They don't have the time or resources to get a truck in for repairs. Your business sends a team of two to drive to their business and pick up the customer's truck and drive it back to your shop for repairs. The customer sees this as unique and Remarkable and has five more trucks repaired at your shop.

## Transportation Business

You have a truck/trailer going to a remote location on your scheduled run that only happens every two months. One of your customers calls your office and asks for two large items that you don't stock (e.g., a fridge and a water cooler). Your sales representative offers to buy the products at a local store and picks them up in his own vehicle. He then gets them on the trailer so that they can be delivered to the remote location. Some would say this is Remarkable Service.

## Automotive Dealership

A customer from a competing dealership calls and complains that the service they have been receiving was very poor and they want to see if your dealerships is any better. Your dealership offers to pick up the customer to wow her and build trust.  Many would suggest that this is Remarkable Service.

## Waste Management Service

One of your customers needs a waste bin on an oil and gas site that is 90 minutes away. It's 2:00 p.m. on the Friday before a long weekend, and there is no scheduled run to this area for 2 more weeks. One of your sales representatives loads a bin on his pickup truck that afternoon and offers to deliver it first thing Saturday morning. Some would say this is Remarkable Service.

## Hotel

It's 4:45 a.m. and one of your guests calls down to the front desk as there is no coffee machine in the room. A young man taking the call offers to bring a machine to your guest's room right away.

He asks what their favourite coffee is and if they would like something to eat. The guest shares his wish list for coffee and an early-morning breakfast. Ten minutes later the machine arrives along with the requested coffee and food. When the guest checks out he is pleasantly surprised to discover he has not been charged a room service fee. He recommends your hotel to his family and friends. Some would suggest that this is Remarkable Service.

## Crane Company

You do a large lift job for a customer and damage an expensive piece of their equipment because your crane didn't have the lift capacity for this particular job. You drive back to your shop that is four hours away and bring out a larger crane the next day to finish the lift and make it right. You don't bill your customer for the additional lift and significantly reduce the bill on the original lift. Some may say that this is Remarkable Service.

# Leaders Must Face the Music

My friend Tim James (VP at Edmonton-based Clark Builders) and I met to enjoy a lunch and catch up at the Cactus Club on Jasper Avenue in Edmonton, which is one of our usual meeting spots. It is always great to visit with Tim and it usually takes us time to order as we both have so much to talk about. About 5 minutes into our visit, the music really started to get loud. While Tim and I aren't kids anymore, we do appreciate great music but when it is so loud that you have to almost yell in each other's ear, then it's annoying. Tim hopped off his chair, walked over to one of the staff at the counter and returned after a quick conversation. Tim is a professional and his concerns would surely garner some attention. As we continued to strain through our "loud" conversation with the music still booming, our server came by to tell us that the manager told her the music is at this standard level over lunch and that there was nothing she could do. I quickly replied, "*What about your customers?*" She seemed confused and had no reply. I went on to say, "*Why don't you send your manager to our table?*" She sheepishly replied, "*Ok.*" Within a minute her manager stopped by our table. "*Gentlemen, I apologize that the music seems too loud for you. I have tried to adjust our speakers in this area, but let me try again and see if I can resolve the issue for you.*" We were impressed and replied "*Hey, we come here often and love your restaurant. We aren't grumpy old guys looking to complain, but it's hard to have a good visit when you have to yell over the music.*" He replied that he totally understood. A few minutes later he came back and asked if the volume was any better. Tim and I agreed that it was better and thanked him for his help. To our pleasant surprise, he also personally delivered our meals and again asked if everything was going well and if the music was still at a comfortable volume. We both agreed that things were much better. When we had finished our meal, the manager stopped by with the bill, thanked us for bringing the issue to his attention and totally surprised us by saying, "*This lunch is on me, gents.*" Wow! Were we delighted! It was great that he resolved our issue, but he went above and beyond. He then asked for our business cards and offered that if we ever needed anything, to connect with him directly. In fact, within four hours of our visit, I received an email from him, which read:

*Hi Mike. Pleasure meeting you earlier today and thank you for your feedback on the music. Please feel free to contact me directly for future reservations or requests.*
*Sincerely,*
*Kyle - Regional Store Manager*
*Cactus Club Cafe*

Kyle gets it and definitely provides Remarkable Service. Kudos to Kyle and his tremendous leadership, which was music to our ears!!

# Hurry, Don't be Late!

JD was in Grande Prairie, Alberta for his regular business trip, meeting with his team and colleagues.

It was a snowy and frigid January day in Northern Alberta and JD was finishing up his business meetings and planning to head to the airport to fly home to British Columbia. Here is JD's story of Remarkable Service.

Today, as I was sitting in the Grande Prairie branch packing up my gear to make my evening flight and chatting with a colleague, I noticed my West Jet boarding pass alert pop up on my screen. It advised me that my plane was boarding at 2:55. All good, except I had not compensated for the 1 hour time change, and it was now 3pm.

I ran for the door, hopped in the car and bolted down the slippery highway towards the airport, pretty convinced I was going to be spending another night at the Pomeroy Hotel.

A call came into my cell and even though I was driving 20km over the speed limit on icy, winter road conditions, I answered the phone (I think Mike Mack's communication profile project had identified I also like to multi-task.) It was Megan from West Jet asking if I would be making the flight today. I explained to Megan (thinking she was from a call centre in Calgary) *"Absolutely Megan, I am just pulling into the airport and will be right there*". (I was still on the main highway outside the dealership, at least 10 minutes away.)

As I completed a perfectly executed 4-wheel drift into the Avis parking stall at the airport and quickly ran through the parking lot, a young girl in West Jet garb, with a big smile said *"James is that you?"* She looked quite cold as I think she had been standing out there for about 9 minutes and 50 seconds. It was Megan!!

She said, *"I think we can still make the fligh*t" and asked what I needed to do. I told her I needed to return the rental car, wherein she took the keys and said, *"I've got that handled for you, go to the gate."*

She had arranged for me to get through security ahead of the line-up and I darted to the gate.

At the gate, two ladies greeted me with big smiles and a *"James!! You are never late for your flights!"* and promptly walked me out to the tarmac.

As we were walking I apologized profusely for being late and they explained absolutely no problem on their part, but they advised some of the other passengers might be giving me the 'stink eye', as they had all been boarded for about 20 minutes. Let's just say that the beer I had wasn't the chilliest part of the flight.

Long story short, I take back what I previously said about West Jet. They are Remarkable and I will be sending an email to their customer service department and telling my friends of this Remarkable experience!!

For those colleagues that were not there during our team meeting in Alberta, part of the Mike Mack presentation included a comparison between Air Canada and West Jet.

I was a little vocal in regard to my changing opinion I once had of West Jet and how a few years ago – if you had asked me if they were Remarkable – I would have vehemently said yes, they are! But in the last few years I had noticed West Jet inching closer and closer to Air Canada (and not in a Remarkable way). Thanks to this great experience, they are now back to their Remarkable ways. Thanks West Jet!!"

I am grateful that JD contributed his Remarkable Service story to my book. Here's another positive airline story from my friend, Dr. Douglas Miller.

"We've all been there... inexplicable flight delays leading to unbearably tight connections in a big, busy airport. All part of today's business air travel alt reality. So, on a delayed flight from New York into Atlanta, we frequent fliers were assured by the on-board staff that our connections were aware and that we should all rapidly head to our gates. Arriving at one end of Terminal D fifteen minutes before my connection departure time, I dodged other travelers and sprinted to my gate. I arrived ten minutes before departure, and was greeted by a closed boarding gate door and no staff. The electronic sign flashed 'Boarding'... Quietly, I fumed. The boarding agent finally emerged, and informed me that the flight was 'Closed', and that my upgraded seat had been given away to another passenger. I protested, in vain, about the airline's multiple failures. The boarding agent had no excuses or answers. But then, unpredictably, she walked me across the terminal to a nearby gate, where a delayed flight to my destination was 'Boarding'. She unlocked the door to the ramp, and returned with the news that "I can get you on this flight... They have a seat." Despite a balky computer, she deftly processed my ticket transfer, handed me a new boarding pass, and shepherded me down the ramp. I could have hugged her! But instead, I shook her hand, thanked her profusely, and went on my way. Rarely does one see an agent of a big monopoly corporation who, when confronted with a very unhappy customer at the end of a long day in the travel trenches, completely save the day with a show of such personal initiative. It almost gives me enough faith to take my next flight."

# Cash or Credit?

This Remarkable Service story was shared by the legendary Patricia Fripp.

Patricia is a Hall of Fame keynote speaker, executive speech coach, sales presentation trainer and online learning expert. Patricia was the first female president of the over 3,500 member National Speakers Association. *Kiplinger's Personal Finance* wrote that one of the best investments in yourself is to learn presentation skills from Patricia Fripp. This author is a smart man ( ☺ ) who is taking advantage of her advice. **www.fripp.com**

Patricia recently became my speaking coach, and I am delighted with her support and proven expertise, as well as her contribution to my book.

Patricia: A number of years back I was in Phoenix, Arizona, speaking for American Express. A young man, Steve Hudson, had the job of looking after me. He told me that the week before he had gone to a big high-end mall to buy 10 boxes of chocolates for his staff as a thank you for a project they had finished. This was his experience.

Steve: Patricia, there were two candy stores in the mall, almost opposite one another. I popped my head around the door of the first one and said, "*Excuse me, do you accept American Express?*" She said, "*Yes.*" So, I wandered in, chose ten boxes of chocolates, and put them on the counter. There I saw the VISA and MasterCard logos but not American Express. I looked at my boxes of chocolates, about a $150 purchase, which I think has to be pretty big for a candy store. Then I turned around, looked across at the other candy store, and recognized the American Express logo in the distance. I said to the cashier, "*You know, I work for American Express. I know you accept our card, but you don't advertise us, and the other store does. I have to take my business over there.*" She nodded; she understood. Fortunately, however, a 16-year-old kid, working after school for minimum wage, wiping the counters and stocking the shelves, overheard this interaction. He said, "*Hold on, sir! Hold on!*" He raced out of the store and across the mall to the other candy store, picked up an American Express application, raced back, cut out the American Express logo, and taped it to the register. He smiled as he said, "*Sir, is that good enough?*"

Patricia: That young man was acting as if his name was on the door. He took the initiative. He creatively removed the obstacle. He saved the customer!

Food for thought:

How many of your employees would do what this young man did?

Would you support his actions?

What caused this young man to do what he did?

Was he trained to do it, or was it just common sense?

# What a Blood Clot Taught Me About Customer Service

Over a year ago, my friend Chad Griffiths woke up to the sound of singing birds and the warmth of the sun that crept through his bedroom blinds. Here's Chad scary story.

Spring is an amazing time in Edmonton, but this particular spring morning my wife was dialling 911 as I was struggling to breathe.

Two days earlier I had had elective foot surgery. I had booked the surgery months in advance, so I had time to prepare for the 6 - 8 week recovery time. My wife had booked time off work, and my co-workers were prepared to assist with my day-to-day responsibilities. I had even practiced on crutches and bought a wheelchair for longer distances.

The surgeon had warned me about potential complications, but since it was fairly routine surgery, I wasn't ready for what came next.

That morning I thought I was having a heart attack. Adding to the pressure on my chest, the painkillers from the night before had worn off and my foot was throbbing under the weight and heat of the cast. I lay in bed in considerable discomfort as two firefighters came into the bedroom. Two more firefighters joined. Two paramedics walked in moments later, followed by two more. A neighbour later told me he thought it was a training exercise for the paramedics and fire department. With four firefighters and four paramedics coming and going, they quickly decided to take me to the hospital. Given my broken foot and difficulty breathing, the task of getting from the second floor of our house down to the ambulance was a bit daunting. The paramedics were sympathetic to these challenges and went out of their way to accommodate me hobbling down the stairs, out the door, and onto the gurney. They helped my wife feel more at ease and were patient with me through the whole ordeal.

At the hospital, a litany of tests showed I had a blood clot in my lungs. The doctor explained that a clot likely developed in my foot, known as a deep vein thrombosis. It subsequently traveled and lodged in my lungs, making it a pulmonary embolism. I was immediately given an anticoagulant injection and informed I would need to take blood thinners for the next few months. A haematologist would later explain that I was fortunate that the clot ended up in my lungs, as a clot could also make its way to the heart or brain and have significantly worse results. While I am blessed to have avoided a more serious clot, it was still hell for me at the time. Following my discharge from the hospital, I had further complications including severe back spasms and urinary retention with an accompanying catheter. This compounded the pain from my surgically repaired foot and the blood clot in my lungs.

Combined, these complications forced me to spend over 50 hours in a hospital post-surgery.

Life didn't get a whole lot easier when I finally settled at home. At rock bottom, I slipped while crutching to the bathroom and I literally - and emotionally - hit the floor. I was lying on the ground with a surgically repaired  foot, a back spasm, and with a urine bag strewn around one of the crutches. I felt broken at that moment, but my wife Lauren came and physically helped me up. Equally important, she helped lift my spirits. Friends and family offered assistance wherever possible and my kids would lay with me in bed so I could read them stories. The support I received and the little moments with my kids helped me fight off depression. When I finish writing this, I'm going to give them each a hug.

After the surgery, I saw multiple doctors, specialists, paramedics, nurses, x-ray technicians, physio and massage therapists. An interesting observation I had during my recovery was how many of these medical and health professionals provided Remarkable Service. Without me asking, both the physio and massage therapists offered to come to my house to provide treatment. I doubt either of them gives regular house calls, but they understood my situation and jumped at the chance to provide an unexpected service. The doctors, nurses, and paramedics were consistently kind and patient, going out of their way to help make me comfortable. Even something as basic as an x-ray becomes more complicated when you have a foot in a cast, a back spasm, and a catheter, and the technicians I met all epitomized great service as they recognized the challenge.

It would be easy to suggest these professionals were just doing their job, but I believe certain people go above and beyond simple expectations. I for one am very grateful they went beyond being average as it made my difficult journey much easier.

I've worked in customer service for the last 20 years, yet this recent experience highlighted a trait in those who provide Remarkable Service: They put their focus entirely and selflessly on the person they are helping.

*Chad Griffiths, SIOR, CCIM, is a Partner with NAI Commercial Real Estate Inc. in Edmonton, Alberta,* **www.edmontoncommercial.com** *. He is also a contributor to Forbes Real Estate Council.*

# Road to Remarkable

Being in the luxury car business may look glamorous, but it is not an easy business. With stiff competition and high customer expectations, you must constantly take two steps forward and sometimes take a step back - to see what needs tweaking in the business to keep customers coming in the door. So how can you create Remarkable Service?

According to Gerry Lorente, Dealer Principal at Bavaria BMW in Edmonton, Alberta Canada, you must make it part of your dealership's culture and constantly strive to be better every day. Bavaria BMW has been operating in Edmonton, Alberta for 30 years. It hasn't always been known as a place for Remarkable Customer Service, but that has changed over the past few years.

In a discussion with Gerry, I asked him what he focuses on to keep customer service top of mind with his team and how the shift in improving customer service has shown steady improvement. Gerry commented that he "constantly invests in his people."

This may seem like standard practice, but the time and dollars associated with this area are significant to say the least. Your people are a value asset and always the first point of contact when a customer pulls up to the service bay or walks in the showroom door to have a look at a car. An aspect that has impressed me is the look and feel of their state of the art training room. When you walk in, you will see a steady flow of inspirational quotes that are all about people and customers. The core values of Bavaria BMW are listed on the wall as well:

Bavaria BMW

### Five Core Values

#### Attitude
Team members must always have a positive attitude when dealing with customers and colleagues. The conduct of an individual affects the environment as a whole.

#### Trust
We must uphold trust in all professional interactions, including customers, and teammates, demonstrated through both our words and actions.

#### Respect
In order to gain respect, always treat others with respect. We must show respect to individuals, their privacy, the workplace, and property.

#### Honesty
We must be honest and up front in all matters pertaining to ourselves, our teammates, and our customers.

#### Responsibility
Team members are accountable for their own actions. Successfully achieving goals is the result of individuals being responsible for both themselves and the team.

It is Gerry's belief that every company has to stand for something and commit to demonstrating value to the customer every single day.

While the BMW brand carries a lot of history and class from a performance perspective, it is a tall order to continually wow the BMW customer.

Customer challenges will happen, but as Gerry states, "Ultimately, it's how you take care of your customer."

Bavaria recognizes that taking care of their customers extends to taking care of their community as well. A few years ago, the dealership decided to change the direction of their business and focus more on the community and giving back. Charity fundraisers and summer barbeques with customers and non-profit organizations fuelled them to make a difference. In 2017, Bavaria BMW organized over 70 events in the city.

"Supporting events like the PTSD Fall Fashion Show and helping contribute thousands of dollars feels great," says Gerry.

It is clear that giving back in this Remarkable way has had a positive impact on the Bavaria BMW team and drives them to new heights in how they look to deliver Remarkable Service to their customers.

In a conversation with Kingsley Fung, who has been with Bavaria BMW for over 5 years in several roles, including Director of Finance and now Sales Manager, I asked him, "When you think about service, what does 'Remarkable' mean in the customer's eyes?"

"Offering a great experience that is unforgettable where we exceed their expectations. But this doesn't always happen. I believe there are some challenges and small issues for sure. I think a lot of the time, when a customer has a bad experience, the first thing that comes to mind is always miscommunication between departments. It takes ongoing work to be regarded as Remarkable in our customers' eyes. If we have good communication, it will be a good experience. Bad communication will be a bad experience. I think I've found that communication is one of the main areas that require our continued focus on the road to Remarkable Service."

I then asked Kingsley, "Let's look down the road, and 12 months from now we listen to what everyone is saying about Bavaria BMW. What are they saying?"

"I would hope that they say that we go above and beyond every time for our customer needs, even though it is very difficult to satisfy all of them. We definitely need to try more than a lot of other dealerships do. Everyone on our team is genuine, friendly and outgoing, and it's like a one big family at Bavaria BMW. Less corporate feeling, and more about the team and our customers.

Customers walk through the door and usually have a good feeling right off the bat compared with other dealerships, at least that is what many customers have told me."

This is a vision that is echoed by Bavaria's Parts Manager, Rich Laliberte, one of the veteran leaders at Bavaria BMW, who is approaching his 10th year at the dealership. I had the opportunity to chat with him and get his take on providing Remarkable Service.

Rich, in the world of Parts, when you think about taking care of your customers, what's your number one priority every day?

"Basically, that they walk out the door with a smile on their face and know that they received value for what they bought."

How do they measure value? You are not the cheapest in town; BMW is an elite brand.

"Service knowledge and how we deal with the customer. We know them and call them by their first name, so it's the little things that make the bigger difference sometimes. It's not always based on dollars."

In your world, is it more challenging during certain times of the year, like the fall to winter season?

"Yes, for sure, just like Christmas, we know tougher weather and driving conditions come every year. We can prepare as much as we can, but it's always a different dynamic because every customer has different needs and wants, but ultimately, we just facilitate what they need. So, it's always interesting because it's the same, but it's always different."

What gives you the greatest satisfaction from a customer service perspective?

"I have been at Bavaria BMW for almost 10 years so I've seen a lot. For me, it's simple. It's just the customer walking away with a smile, knowing that they'll be coming back, and it's not even a thought in their mind. And I always look at that as a million dollar customer because that one customer that's satisfied will talk to their friends, their coworkers, their relatives, and family, so it just keeps going on and on, like a domino effect. "

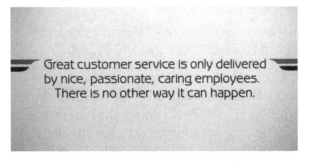

Great customer service is only delivered by nice, passionate, caring employees. There is no other way it can happen.

In the Parts Department, you also have internal customers, so keeping service, and sales in some cases, happy, can be a challenge. How do you make that happen and maintain focus on that internal customer?

"In our business, time is the death of everything for internal, so as long as I can be within the 48 to 72-hour period that everything is flowing for them, and I'm not stalling them out, then I know their customer, 'our customer', is going to be happy. I don't get to see it, but that's ultimately my goal for that."

In any dealership the Service Department handles many of the customer challenges and in speaking with Service Manager, Garrett Dyck, he offered his perspective on the highs and lows of being face-to-face with customer service issues.

How do you handle the demands of our changing season like the recent early snowfall where 3 to 5 inches hit the roads and your customers have trouble driving?

"Well, a week ago, we set out having approximately sixty percent of our customers booked in for their snow tire change over. That kind of got turned upside down with Mother Nature's early snow dump. While it pretty much snows every year by Halloween, almost without question, every year, it seems to catch a number of people off guard. So as much preparation and planning as we do, as soon as that snow hits the road, it creates a big tailspin for us. Customer expectation is at an all-time high regardless of what you do, whether it's a restaurant, a hotel, or a luxury car business, that customer's expectation is through the roof on how they're dealt with and treated, both prior to the appointment, and then during the appointment, and then obviously after the appointment. We try to offer as many high-quality services as possible. And then when something like this happens, when Mother Nature blesses us with lovely weather, it changes our game. The most prepared you can be is still not prepared enough, especially when you have close to 600 sets of tires stored for customers, and they're all trying to get on in a finite amount of time."

As one of the leaders at Bavaria BMW, how do you instill Remarkable Service in your team and have them understand that customers are not always going to be happy in hectic times like that?

"I guess, on first snowfall day or when we see the forecast hit certain degrees of temperature, you rally the troops by telling them to get a good night's sleep, because you know the next day is going to be busy. We just try to get up early the next morning because we know it's going to be busy and the phones will ring off the hook and everything will move at a super fast pace. We must empathize with all those customers who are in panic mode when the roads are slippery and they need our help. Everyone's busy so for us, it's about trying to expand what we do and it's not one or two people, it's actually the entire team, so it's every service technician in the shop coming 15 minutes earlier and staying 15 minutes later. We run extended service hours on the weekends or even some of the nights."

Garrett continues: "Hey, when it first snowed, you're darn right the lady or the gentleman sitting across the desk was white-knuckling it on the way here. Yeah, she was on four summer tires, maybe, in the middle of winter. Yeah, maybe they didn't plan properly but I can appreciate that. I wouldn't want my daughter or wife driving around if I made an appointment and it snowed earlier than my appointment, so, you really have to take that into consideration and help the customer."

I've titled this chapter of the book 'Road to Remarkable' and, acknowledging the time that you've been working at the dealership, you can perhaps agree that, at times, it hasn't always been Remarkable. So what's your focus, that the customers out there in the Edmonton marketplace are remarking in a highly favorable way, whether that's through CSI - Customer Service Index or Google reviews? What is the goal for you in that regard, to have customers say good things because they mean it?

"People can buy CSI at any point. Then when you tie dollars and cents to pretty much anything in any industry, the reaction is not necessarily genuine. It's a false positive, essentially. When I came to work at the dealership four years ago, there was no false positive. It was just negative. There was very little light at the end of the tunnel and it took our team a long time to turn the ship around. And before we even gave it gas, we just needed to essentially stop one direction before we could move in another. We stayed true to our course, because our service levels needed to improve. It was not easy, but my team and I didn't get discouraged on negative feedback. We are accepting of the feedback we get, positive and negative, but rather than give ourselves a score, like 5 stars with no comments, I wanted 1 star with a bunch of comments. And not malicious, just 'Listen, you need to do this better,' so that we could turn around and say, 'Okay, that makes sense; businesswise, this makes sense.' Maybe that translates into hiring another body or a different shuttle driver or having extended hours, but the customer's feedback is essentially what's going to drive our business.

In the automotive industry, you can argue that the biggest pressure side of the business lies in the service department. The honeymoon's great on the front end. The customer buys a new car but as soon as there's an issue, he's going to be less happy. How do you take that pressure and do something that's positive and sustainable from a customer's perspective?

"I look back on my path on the service end and to deal with broken cars as opposed to brand new shiny ones is definitely a bigger challenge. I think there's a challenge in selling new vehicles or used vehicles, but there's definitely a challenge when they break down and it's no longer safe to drive. The 'Road to Remarkable' title is very fitting for us, as our biggest focus right now is just making sure that that customer's expectations are met, and sometimes just setting that expectation right from the get-go is where it has to be done. For example, working with the sales team as a start in getting to know the customer, to understand the vehicles they have. We focus on training our advisors to make sure that they know what goes on, and at what intervals, and to prevent some of these breakdowns from happening."

Garrett continues: "We need to look at retention, and repeat business, and selling the second vehicle. I think one of the industry things is 'Sales sells the first car, and service sells every one after that'. Today's standard is tomorrow's expectation. Something that we do today that we feel improves the level of service, like a car wash. Now, if you went in and didn't get your car washed, well, you would be disappointed. Yes, it's a free service, however, it started with one person offering it. Now everyone offers it. Now it must include vacuuming the car, then it'll be detailing the car. Eventually, you haven't even exceeded expectations anymore. Now, you've just met the expectation."

To build trust with customers, at times have you seen, for yourself or your team, that you've had to be vulnerable and acknowledge, "Hey, we made a mistake," which is not easy to do, to acknowledge it. But what does that vulnerability-based trust look like in your world and your team, more importantly?

"The Service Advisors have done the best job at that. They're the ones that are on the forefront in the trenches with the customer. My advisors see between 8 and 15 people a day, so I think they've done a better job of admitting fault when we've made mistakes. And we really look for feedback from the customer, right from the get-go and when a customer comes in and gives us that feedback, we try to use that to fix the concern. It can be a little bit reactionary, but eventually, after reacting to some instances, you then get to put in a process that makes it preventative so that it doesn't happen again."

"All departments must operate as a cohesive team; Sales, Service, Parts, Finance and Accounting working to serve the best interest of their values, the customers and the overall dealership. They must trust that each department will always do their part to support the collective team. It's the only way we can compete and how we can earn the customer's business. Our people try to work and act with high moral standards, but we are human and we can make mistakes. It's not always easy. Adversity that occurs sometimes is a challenge, but what I continually try to instill in our service team is that it can make us stronger."

OUR COMMITMENT

We must always treat our customers like invited guests to our home every day, every time without fail, with no exception. We would be nothing without our valued customers.

Gerry Lorente
Dealer Principal

Gerry Lorente acknowledges that Bavaria BMW has come a long way over the years, but the 'Road to Remarkable' is an ongoing journey and one he is prepared to take. "Our customers matter to us a great deal and we must constantly improve and be better. We appreciate them in the good times but also when they get frustrated with our service. It's our responsibility to make it right and enhance their overall customer service experience."

I am delighted to have the team at Bavaria BMW as a valued customer of mine and thank them for taking the time to contribute to this chapter of my book.  Learn more about Bavaria BMW: www.bavariabmw.ca

# Why More Businesses Don't Create Remarkable Service

There are a number of reasons why more businesses don't provide Remarkable Service. First of all, they don't pay enough attention to improving their service or building stronger relationships with their customers. (It's like a marriage that ends, and one spouse says to the other, "*It's wasn't bad, but I really don't feel like making it good again.*") It's easy to get complacent when no one is really too unhappy about anything. Often times, business owners and their employees go about business and assume that all is well (or at least HOPE that all is well). If it isn't going well, they may avoid talking about it, as it only happens once in a while. Maybe their service isn't bad, but it's definitely not Remarkable.

The other aspect is that businesses are just too busy. Day in and day out, you do your best to support customers, but are we spending enough time working 'on' the business to improve customer service? Most businesses don't spend enough time working 'on' their business. You need to see how your business is delivering service, and ideally see it from your customers' eyes. Working in our business, I am constantly looking at every customer service experience that I encounter. If I go to the gym, and the front desk staff doesn't even look up at me when I walk by, I think, "*You just don't get it.*" This is not hard! Take five-seconds to look at your customer and say, "*Good morning*."

Another reason businesses are not creating Remarkable Service is because they don't invest in training their people. They may not know how to properly train someone in customer service. Everyone must understand what it takes to retain customers. Organizations that do this well have great leaders who see the importance of making their people better. If you want to retain more customers and acquire new customers through your sales process, customer service is a significant catalyst to get you there.

**Don't forget to determine the Lifetime Value of your customer** (i.e. revenue/transactions; transactions/year; revenue/year; # of years that customer will be 'your' customer; customer lifetime value; likelihood of "great" and Remarkable Service keeping your customer).

Do you know the value of your customers in your business?

_____

_____

_____

E.g. I am a customer at a drycleaner. Let's look at the lifetime value of my business to that store as a customer. I spend $30 to $40 in a given week on dry cleaning. If I do that 50 weeks a year, $40/week x 50 weeks = $2,000 of business per year. You get a pretty quick number of what I'm worth to that business as a customer in one year. Now, what if I'm a customer for seven or eight years, like I've been? What if I'm a customer for another 10 years: 10 x $2,000 = $20,000. The lifetime value of one average customer like me, Mike Mack, is valuable, and I want businesses and their employees to understand the lifetime value of all of their customers. Not just the big customers, but the average customers (I say average just based on average revenue/sale) and the smaller customers who still spend some valued money within a business, which is important.

Another question that I spend a lot of time addressing is, "What is the cost of poor service?" There are many examples, such as an unreturned phone call for a quote on a particular product. I can think of an example where I had requested a quote on a $400 part for my vehicle, and the business never called me back with a price. The cost of poor service in that case was the entire amount of the purchase -$400. That company didn't get my business. Their competitor did!

I want your business to understand what the cost of poor service can be and how it can impact your bottom-line!

# Orion Environmental Cares About Customers

Orion Environmental was a valued customer of mine in 2017 and I was so impressed with their commitment to customer service, that I asked for them to share a story for my book. This is based on an interview with one of the owners, Steve Masse. **www.orionenviro.ca**

About ten days ago, we were awarded the Tourmaline contract to haul fluid for a frac-program; a fairly large volume and a small window of opportunity to get the fluid in. We spent a bit of time prior to the job setting up some efficiencies with boat stations, directions, road signage, proper preparation. We had enough lead-time to do that. We lined up the appropriate amount of equipment to handle the job in about a 90% capacity of what we are capable of. Everything went off excellent. Our preparation worked great, our operators were rested and prepared, the weather cooperated and we finished the five-day job in three and a half days. The whole time we were doing the job, the customer was skeptical that anybody would be able to keep up with their demand. We far exceeded what they required just by being prepared. The end result was a very happy client and a very successful and profitable job for the company. In turn, the reputation of our company rippled through the rest of the Tourmaline organization and we received calls from a number of different field consultants to assist them with their smaller projects. We were asked to bid on the next high demand, large volume job, which unfortunately our prior commitments didn't allow us to have enough equipment and man-power, so we graciously declined the job. Tourmaline respectfully accepted our answer, appreciative that we would be upfront with them and admit we just couldn't pull the next one off. We knew that we had to allow another competitor to do that job, because if we attempted to, we would most likely fail. They contacted several of their other vendors and then called us back and said none of their vendors felt that they could handle the project. We suggested we team up with one of the other vendors and share the workload together. That is what we are doing right now. We are out here doing this large project sharing it with one of their other vendors that we work with and compete against in other areas.

We have spoken directly to the supervisors of the other vending company and we both  agreed we'd put our best foot forward and do the best we can for our customer, so we are doing a cooperative job here now. We are working equally the same and will share the load 50/50. We will work together for the big picture, the ultimate goal.

I am most proud of the fact that my management team, my operators and myself really get behind what we do. Whether it is us doing the job solo, or working with another company, at the end of the day we don't show up to fail, we show up to succeed and we put the effort in that's required to make that happen. At the end of the day, we get great satisfaction from accomplishing challenging projects and ultimately supporting our customers.

# No Training Required

On a vacation to Mexico a few years ago, my wife and I decided to go on one of those adventure excursions sold through our resort. It was a full day excursion including ATVing through the jungle, boating and sometimes snorkeling and swimming in the ocean. It sounded like an amazing way to spend the day! The trip was not cheap at $360 USD for the two of us, but the agency booking the excursion did a great job of explaining the day-long trip and we were sold. The next morning, we were up early and eager to start our adventure.

When we left the hotel, we had about a one-hour van ride to reach our destination. We had a tour guide who explained some of the details of our upcoming adventure and everything seemed great. We joined up with the rest of the group where we were all going to get on the ATVs. There were about 23 of us in total. We were going to be driving our ATV side by sides 90 minutes one way into the Mexican jungle, and doing some off-roading. It sounded pretty cool.

As we were preparing to go, our guide needed to make sure that we were all experienced and capable to operate and drive the ATVs, and as such, he was required to do a driving orientation with each driver.

It was now my turn for orientation. The tour guide walked up beside the ATV and said, "*Do you know how to drive?*" I replied "*Yes*", and he said, "*Good.*" Well apparently, that was the end of my driving lessons and we were good to go.

 We headed down the road onto the highway and then onto rougher roads full of potholes and muddy water. We continued on and later learned that this was the "off-roading" portion of the excursion. One passenger of our ATV said to us, "*This isn't off-roading, this is just driving on a very bad road.*" LOL!

In light of the fact that we had passengers in the back seat of our ATV, I was driving a little bit slower. I asked if they were open to going a little bit faster even though we would probably get wet and muddy driving through the water and they said "*Go for it!*"

As we entered our third or fourth major mud waterhole, all of a sudden, the engine was sputtering and we were crawling along at a snail's pace. The engine light came on and we thought, "*Great, we are not going to enjoy the day ahead!!*"

Inevitably, the engine stalled and we had to dry it out for a while. Parked in the middle of nowhere, with strange animal noises in the trees and several snakes slithering near the empty road, one thing became very evident; no one was waiting for us, as there was no tour guide behind us (even though this had been promised at the start of our tour). The entire group, including the two guides, were way ahead of us, and we had no way of knowing by how much. Thirty to forty-five minutes later we were back on the road, rolling along and going as fast as we could to try to catch up. Finally, we came upon the remainder of the group while they were stopped for some sightseeing. We explained that we'd had vehicle problems, but no one seemed to care too much about that.

We had another 30-minute drive before stopping for lunch and made it without any further problems. When we arrived at a small village where we were going to have lunch, I decided to pull the lead tour guide member aside and explain to him about our issue and concerns for our return trip. Somewhere in our conversation, I asked how long he had been doing this job, and he said, **"I've been on the job four days."** Wow! Four days doesn't seem like a lot of time, and my guess was he'd had little to zero training and orientation. It was pretty obvious. His leadership and customer-service savvy were non-existent. Apparently, we weren't the only customers that were upset. We could overhear some people from another country challenging the lead tour guide about what was going on. He didn't seem to care too much about their concerns either.

Now it was time to board the boats for some touring and we teamed up with a German couple who were both doctors. They definitely weren't big fans of the tour experience either. The weather was amazing and we were thrilled to see some dolphins and turtles, which proved to be a highlight of the trip. Watching these beautiful creatures from the boat made us even more excited to go snorkelling. However, this was not to be, as the lead guide stunned us by saying: "*Unfortunately, we can't go snorkelling today!*" Everyone was shocked and angry, asking him why. He said, "*We have certain regulations, and we can't go snorkelling today.*" I thought to myself, we can't go snorkelling today because it's nice and sunny, the water's calm, or was there another reason?

As I think back, I'm not even certain there was any snorkelling gear anywhere on any boat. Were we ever really going to go snorkelling?... We would never know.

It was now time to head back to land and drive our ATVs the two-hour-plus trek back to where our van was parked, through the jungle and through the rough roads, mud and water. Would our ATV make it?

To add to our concerns the sun was starting to go down and we still had two hours of driving ahead. If we continued to have ATV problems, we were going to be really behind and the reality was, no one was going to wait for us. In fact, no one would likely care. The German couple I mentioned earlier must have trusted us as they decided to ride back with us. They were chatting with each other and voicing their concerns in German. It was somewhat cute as my wife can speak German and understood everything that they were saying.

As predicted, we did have more engine problems but we had a different strategy this time. We drove very slowly through the water to try to prevent our engine from stalling, but when the road was dry and rough, we went full tilt to try to make up some time.

Our final 35 minutes of the tour ended in a small village and we had to make our way through town, but here's the catch: No one was around again, and **we were all by ourselves in the dark, not really knowing exactly where we had to go.** We had to guess which road to take. Was this the kind of adventure that we were looking for?

We finally made it back to the starting point where our tour van was parked and we had to drop off the ATV. By this time, most of the group had already gone.

There was a small group remaining, including the Spanish-speaking tourists, and they were ripping into the lead tour guide along with his boss, who was at the checkpoint. We heard the word **refund** and thought, "REFUND? Yeah, right, like they are going to give us a refund ... not likely." But as a few people continued to argue with them, they started to buckle. A young woman who was obviously part of the tour group was trying to calm down the customers and resolve the situation with some possible solutions.

She said to us, "*You are going to have to contact your agent back at your resort to get a refund.*"

I decided to approach her in a less aggressive manner and asked in a calm voice, "*Please explain to us exactly how that's going to happen and how we are going to get a refund?*"

She seemed stunned by the question and her stutter-step response suggested she really didn't have a plan. She looked at all of us and said, "*I will call them now.*" To make sure that she was calling the agency back at the resort, we went into her trailer as well and listened to her phone call. While it was in Spanish, I relied on the tourists who spoke Spanish to understand exactly what was being said. After the call several groups actually started to receive refunds. Now it was our turn. I stood patiently and waited as she handed me over $360 in cold, hard U.S. cash. I was surprised that we actually got our money back. When I headed back to the tour van before we drove back to our resort, I told our new German friends about the refund and they too went in to negotiate and also came back with a pocket full of cash. As we were preparing to leave, I asked the lead tour guide about what he would do differently for the next tour. He replied, "*I don't know or care because I am quitting tonight.*"

This particular trip proved to be somewhat challenging and even potentially dangerous, but ironically, it gave us a lot to talk about when we returned from our vacation. It definitely made for some interesting content for this book to illustrate the power of training and effectively teaching and coaching people on how to deal with challenging situations, difficult customers, and how to be a leader when it comes to customer service.

While this story took place in Mexico, it could have happened in Canada, the United States, or anywhere else in the world. The point is: If you don't train your people and prepare them for effective customer service and give your customers good service experiences, your business will have major problems, including a loss of business.

The reality is that not all of us are going on excursions like this, but many of us go to stores or places of business every day. Whether it's the grocery store, the dry cleaner, the bank, or the car dealership, it doesn't matter. Are the employees of those companies trained to serve you? Do they **leave you in the dark and on your own?** What about your business? Is your team really trained?

As I wrote this story about our Mexican adventure, it really hit me! While this story is true, and even a bit humorous, the sad reality is this type of experience is a daily occurrence for many businesses. It was a real eye-opener.

Does your business overpromise and under-deliver?

Are you guilty for a lack of communication to your customers and keeping them in the dark?

How do you show that you really care about your customer's experience?

In my experience, this happens far too often, and the only thing that is Remarkable is the story that is told by the disappointed customer - **The Remarkably Bad Story about Service!** Let's hope it is not a bad story about your business or mine!

Is hiring right and training well a big deal?

A few years ago, I was speaking to a business connection of mine, who is a very well respected business owner in Western Canada. He is able to travel a lot and enjoys life while his business continues to thrive in the good times and in the more challenging times. He told me, "*Mike, I have the best people in the world working for our business, and I only hire the best.*" While it is hard to verify if he actually has the 'best' people in the world, one thing is hard to deny: his business thrives all the time and has been around for many, many years. If you want the best, don't rush the hiring process!

Food for thought: Many strong and forward-thinking business owners and leaders should consider that when a downturn occurs, it's the time to plan to upgrade their talent pool. While this is a tough decision to make, it allows their business a tremendous opportunity to hire when more time is allowed in the process and they have the ability to hire better people and ideally the best people, simply because more of them may be available in the market.

While this may seem like a cold and unfair decision, it is a very important decision for their business and the future. If someone on your team isn't coachable or they don't fit into your corporate culture, why keep them? You deserve better and so do your customers!

Let's compare it to sports. Hockey teams do this all the time. When a strong team is making a run for the playoffs and ideally achieve their desired goal of a Stanley Cup, they trade players (i.e. upgrade the talent pool). They want the best players on their team to allow them the opportunity to achieve maximum success. This holds true with some talented players that aren't 'team players'. It's all about them and less about the team. They may need to go as they are a cancer to the business and can impact the entire team. Business leaders should think the same way. If your business plans on keeping your doors open for the long-term and continuing to grow and succeed, it is key to upgrade your talent pool with great skills along with desire and attitude, particularly when the talent is more readily available.

One final aspect in this chapter for you to consider:

Businesses usually don't focus on the little things that can make their service Remarkable. Most customers truly appreciate the little things.

The little things can be defined as the habits and behaviors that most customers appreciate.

For example:

Did we greet them by name?

Was the promised delivery time of a product or service ready earlier than expected?

Did we actually take the time to call the customer to tell them that their product was ready early?

Did we smile at the customer and acknowledge them?

They may seem like they aren't that important, but it's the little things that are incredibly significant in any business. When times are good and customers walk in the door and pay any price, your business will likely prosper. However, what happens when times are tough and the economy is challenged with economic hardship, or new and aggressive competitors are opening across the street? Most businesses may resort to cutting prices, but rarely concentrate on improving their customer service.

Did we open the door for our customer?

Did we offer them 'something' that was more than expected?

Did we thank them for coming in, even if they didn't make a purchase?

Here's a simple but Remarkable Service example to illustrate these points.

My wife and I were attending my niece Erin's wedding in Regina, Saskatchewan in July 2017. We were staying at the Hotel Saskatchewan, which is an amazing property with incredible staff. When I called downstairs to ask if I could get some water bottles for the room, the young

man on the phone, said, "*How many do you need?*" I replied, "*Three would be great.*" He said, "*No problem, we will have that up to you in a minute and complimentary for you Mr. Mack.*" Nice, I thought, and literally a minute after I hung up the phone, we had a knock at the door. "*Here is your water, Mr. Mack*". A small thing, but definitely worth remarking about.

Remarkable Service didn't stop there, as we went out for dinner to The Copper Kettle, (@copperkettleyqr) which was across the street from the hotel. We learned that it was one of the oldest restaurants in the city and operated by the same family for over 50 years. After checking out the menu, we agreed to share a 13-inch pizza and salad. A short while later our rock-star server Aman delivered our pizza and salad along with an apology as the chef had prepared a 10-inch pizza instead of our requested 13-inch.

Aman, told us to check the menu for a second pizza of our choice and it would be complimentary.

Such a kind gesture, but please keep in mind we didn't have a tape measure to know that this was only a 10-inch pizza. Many servers might have tried to slip that one past a customer, but not Aman. We thanked him for the offer, but said we would be fine with the smaller pizza. He was quick to say, "*I will make sure you are only charged for the 10.*" As we wrapped up our tasty dinner, Aman asked if we had room for cheesecake which we declined as we were pretty full.

"*How about you share a piece, with fresh saskatoon berries, and it's on me?*" Really, how could we resist? The cheesecake was delicious and the service experience was definitely worthy of mentioning it in my book. I have told this story many times already, and it's another example of a "Remarkable" Service experience.

**Now... for something a lot less tasty than cheesecake.**

A friend of mine from Edmonton bought a second home in Arizona several years ago. Having a home in Arizona is a great way to escape winter in Edmonton. My friend needed to do some shopping to stock his new house with furniture and appliances. He went to a well-known store which I will leave unnamed. He bought a washer and dryer, along with a fridge and a stove package. He arranged delivery while in Arizona because he was only there for one week due to work commitments back home. The delivery truck arrived with the washer, dryer, and stove. *"Where's the fridge?"* my friend asked.

The delivery driver told him, *"I guess they didn't load it on the truck."*

To which my friend responded, "*Well, you have to go back and get it*," and the driver replied, "*We can't because we're fully booked with deliveries*

*this week.*" He immediately called the store and voiced his frustration, and they replied with the same, "*No delivery this week. Sorry.*"

As you can imagine, my friend's frustration hit another level (#%&@), so he drove down to the store and talked to his sales representative. Once again, he was given the same "*No can do*" answer. He escalated his complaint to the store manager. Again, he received the same response. By now his voice was significantly louder and he was asked to keep it down, but he didn't tone it down. He tried to explain that he was only in Arizona for a few days and a delivery next week was simply not an option, but they still didn't want to help. He then asked for a refund on the fridge so that he could go to another store to purchase another one. Astonishingly, they refused to give him his money back! Finally, after more yelling and standing his ground, the manager of the store offered this less-than-Remarkable solution: "*You can rent a truck on your own, we will load the fridge here, but you will have to unload it yourself.*" Unbelievable!! My friend ended up renting a truck and getting his new neighbours to help him unload the fridge in Arizona. Wow! This is not how you service what you sell.

The moral of the story is, don't let your fridge stand alone in the cold. When you buy a fridge and stove, make sure you ask if they are going to be delivered on the same day.

When I hear a story like the one I just described, it frustrates me. I shake my head and think; how would I have handled this customer service disaster if I worked for the store in question? Stories like this demonstrate why I am so passionate about how we can endeavour to help our customers by improving service. Ultimately, it's about *People and Process*. When the right people follow the right process, they are empowered and have the ability to make the right decisions when required!

Now, I know that in some cases customers can be totally unreasonable with their demands, but more often than not, common sense wins the day with your customer. It is my hope that this book will make everyone look at the opportunity to achieve Remarkable Service in a different light and believe that it is actually possible and not that difficult or complicated.

*"We see our customers as invited guests to a party, and we are the hosts. It's our job every day to make every important aspect of the customer service experience a little bit better."*
-Jeff Bezos, Amazon

# Do the Little Things Make a Difference?

The little things may be habits or behaviors that are routine in your business and your employees just do them at the right time and they seem to get joy in doing so. As I have observed over the years, businesses that provide Remarkable Service tend to have happier and more satisfied customers who tell others about their service. Ultimately, that creates stronger loyalty and it can enhance the ability to ask for more referrals or recommendations. As a general rule, their businesses run more smoothly. Their teams are more engaged and helpful, they retain great people, and they are able to weed out the poor performers. They likely have better sales/revenue than a business without Remarkable Service and the customers tend to be less price sensitive when they get Remarkable Service. The team working at a business with Remarkable Service likely has some extra passion to make it all about the customer and they love what they do. Customers tend to remark about the little things, there is usually a consistent theme, and consistency can win the day when it comes to creating Remarkable Service.

My wife, Bonita and I had been planning our dream vacation for over a year and the day finally arrived for us to leave on our two-week holiday in Italy. We planned to arrive in Rome, tour the Vatican, the Colosseum, then head south to the gorgeous Amalfi Coast and visit Positano, the Island of Capri and experience the breath-taking Blue Grotto.

As part of the planning process, we decided to fly Business Class as we would be spending over 12 hours in the air, each way, on our trip. We headed out of Edmonton on a beautiful September day and boarded Air Canada. (I know at times Air Canada has gotten a bad "rap" for service, but specific to Business Class travel, they were Remarkable).

We arrived in Toronto 4 hours later and exited our plane with our carry-on luggage. (Tip: Carry-on only is a must when travelling to Europe, based on travelling expert Rick Steves. We loved the convenience that this brought to our travel experience. Thanks for the tip Rick!).

As we left the ramp, we were greeted by the warm smile of Carol O'Sullivan, Concierge with Air Canada. Our first thought was there might be a problem with our connecting flight to Rome, but Carol was there to tell us about the special Concierge service that Air Canada provides to International travellers in Business Class. She then helped us exit the Domestic Terminal in an expedited fashion by taking us through private access doors. There, we were greeted by a driver and a beautiful BMW sedan to transport us to the International Terminal.

 We were of course delighted by this special treatment and quite impressed to be chauffeured in a BMW 7 Series Sedan!

Carol travelled with us and visited along the drive. She then took us directly to the Air Canada Maple Leaf Lounge and promptly checked-us in.

 Wow, this was truly rock star Remarkable Service! The whole experience only took 7-8 minutes, but Carol and Air Canada saved us at least half an hour that it would have taken us if we had to walk and check-in on our own.

Thank you Carol and Air Canada!

Our trip to Italy was spectacular and we stayed at many great properties and hotels. One hidden gem that is worthy of mention is the Art Commercianti Hotel in the heart of Bologna,

Italy. It is part of the three Bologna Art Hotels. These hotels are a family run and we were delighted to meet one of the Orsi family owners, Ilaria Orsi, in our historical boutique hotel.

Check them out on Instagram: @hotelcommercianti

This hotel is a 12$^{th}$ century building brimming with charm and history. We loved everything about Bologna, especially the hotel and staff that constantly strove to deliver Remarkable Service. A notable example that validates the importance of the doing the "little things" was the morning breakfast and amazing cappuccino to kick-start our day.

On two of the three mornings that we were there, Ilaria **personally** made and served our cappuccino with a smile. I don't know about you, but I'm pretty sure I have never had the hotel owner make or serve me coffee before! We enjoyed a visit with her over breakfast and we chatted about her cute dog Loki who "worked" with Ilaria at the hotel. I was so impressed with the service that I had to capture this story in my book.

*"We always try to do our best to make our guests feel like they are at home. When someone appreciates our work we can only be proud of it."*
– Ilaria Orsi

Not only is Bologna on our list of cities to return to, the Art Commercianti Hotel will be, without question, our accommodation of choice. Our Trip Advisor review echoes these points. ☺

As you can see from a customer's perspective, it really is the 'little things' that can make such a big difference.

Take the time now to think about your business and how the little things can make a difference for your valued customers.

Five little things you do well (i.e. habits and behaviors of your team)

1 _____

2 _____

3 _____

4 _____

5 _____

Five little things you need to improve upon (i.e. habits and behaviors of your team

1 _____

2 _____

3 _____

4 _____

5 _____

# Restaurant Shows Fire Victims Compassion

Here is a heart-warming story shared by a business associate and friend of mine, Jeff Tetz, Partner with Results Canada.
**www.resultsci.com**

All Albertans remember the devastation and carnage left behind after the wild fires in Fort McMurray in May 2016. Whether you knew someone or not, you felt for everyone affected and displaced after the fire hit this hard-working community.

As tough as it was and continues to be for many residents of Fort McMurray, there were  many random acts of kindness. Some were simple goodwill gestures and others took the form of Remarkable Service.

According to Jeff, what is Remarkable about Original Joe's (a customer of Jeff's firm) is they have taken a little bit of a different approach to customer experience and customer service where they didn't start just with training and standardization. They really started from a place of wanting to inspire their employees to behave differently, **not because it's the process manual telling them to do so,** but it's the deeper connection that they feel with their staff and in turn, their staff are compelled to create a connection with all the customers that come in and out of their stores on a daily basis. It didn't happen overnight, but they got very deliberate a few years ago in trying to figure out what their meaningful purpose was and really what their values were. Results Canada played a bit of a roll in helping them gain some clarity on what those elements were. Basically, where they landed is the meaningful purpose to "simply to take care of people." There are no boundaries or limits on that, whether it's a coworker, a family member, taking care of the community and doing a better job of being a good corporate citizen, or taking care of their customers. Original Joe's has spent a lot of time over the course of at least a couple of years at rigorously training and aligning all of their management staff with that core purpose and what it meant and how to use it, and the way that it was going to impact lives and in turn, help them build a better business just by authentically living that purpose. Then the role that the management staff at the store level had to play, in not only trying to do a better job and a more deliberate job of hiring staff that fit that culture and that way of thinking, but then once they were hired, just really building an environment at the store level where that purpose was alive every single day telling stories and undertaking initiatives that were an extension of that purpose. What they are seeing now are some really dramatic changes in experience for customers and financial results have coincided with it. What they've done is they've layered on top of this now, on top of this foundation of purpose and values and culture, a very specific sort of training and they've mandated some policies and procedures that really align with that. As a result, they've had a couple of customer experiences that have gone viral in the last year.

The first was around the Fort McMurray fires back at the beginning of May 2016. It took place in one of Original Joe's locations in the west end of Edmonton. A husband and wife came in for an early evening dinner and as the server was cleaning up their table to go get their bill and get it ready for the next customer, she overheard the husband and wife discussing the fact that their house had burned down the day before in Fort McMurray. So, without even thinking about it, the server goes and grabs the manager and shares the story of what she just heard and in an instant, the manager says by all means let's "comp their bill" which is a small gesture but it's the least we can do. The server takes the bill back and sets it on the table. The wife opens it and starts to openly sob; she's just so appreciative of such a small gesture. The husband takes a photo of the bill and puts it on Facebook and within 72 hours it went viral. **They had over a million interactions with the**

**post.** The story is like in most organizations; you know the difference between doing the right thing and doing things right, you know it's a fine line. A lot of organizations have the right intention and they've got standardized training and policies and procedures; you do this and then you do that, and then you do this. In a normal restaurant environment, because they're so focused on how many customers can we get in and out of the door, how many turns can we get out of that table, it's more about the numbers and the revenue and it's less about the relationships with the customer at certain times. Nobody would've faulted the server if her focus was: okay, this lovely couple that I've just delivered quality food at a reasonable price in a clean environment and an expeditious fashion, I haven't let them down in any of the core expectations of a restaurant experience. If all she would have been focused on was okay, they are done their meal, I have to clean their table within three minutes, I have to get it set for the next group and then as the next group sits down I've got to have their waters on the table within 60 seconds of them sitting down. That's what normally would happen. It wouldn't be wrong, but they are missing the boat. Because Original Joe's has been so deliberate in creating a Remarkable Service environment that really comes from the heart and making meaningful connections, **they've now got business coming in the door** that they never would have had. And it's all because one of their customers put their

Remarkable Service story on social media with a million interactions. In my mind, that's a pretty cool story!!

# Communication and Connection Are Critical

As I have learned from leadership guru and best-selling author, John C. Maxwell, *"connecting is all about others."*

Maxwell stated in his book: *Everyone Communicates - Few Connect, "When you are trying to connect with people, it's not about you - it's about them. If you want to connect with others, you have to get over yourself."*

*"Connecting is the ability to identify with people and relate to them in a way that increases your influence with them,"* says Maxwell.

Three questions people are asking about you, according to John C. Maxwell:

1. Do you care for me?

2. Can you help me?

3. Can I trust you?

These points can play an important role in the pursuit of Remarkable Service and the ability of your business to retain customers.

How do you communicate that you care for your customers?

_____

_____

_____

How do you know if you have connected with a customer?

_____

_____

_____

What are the various ways that you communicate/instill trust with your customers?

_____

_____

_____

# No Worries, Mr. Mack, That Becomes My Problem.

This story took place more than 20 years ago, and I still tell it because it was that Remarkable.

In a previous career within the Financial Services Industry, I spent three years working in Prince George, British Columbia. One of my favourite  restaurants there was called DaMarinos, a delightful little Italian restaurant with amazing food and Remarkable Service. Their spaghetti carbonara was amazing!! One afternoon I took a few hungry colleagues with me who were in town from Vancouver and we arrived just at the beginning of the lunch-hour rush.

As I entered the restaurant, my favorite waiter **Vince** promptly greeted me at the door. "*Good day, Mr. Mack, how are you today?*" I told him I was great.

He responded, "*Do you have reservations?*"

I sheepishly nodded, "*No, sorry, we didn't know our lunch schedule and plans today.*"

He replied, **"*No worries, Mr. Mack, that becomes my problem.*"**

Even to this day, that line is still etched in my mind and it was, and continues to be, one of the most Remarkable statements that I have ever heard from a customer service perspective! I was totally delighted, and that Remarkable Service was so memorable that I continue to tell this story all the time.

What I find interesting when I suggest to our customers and their employees that they need to make their customer's problem their problem, they don't always seem to buy-in to the concept. (The great businesses do.) Here's my point, if you aren't willing to make your customer's problem your problem, then who will? Your competition?

When was the last time that you made your customer's problem your problem? Did you collaborate on a win-win solution? Did you suggest that "we" will figure this out together?

**Customer Service is defined as:**

"*The assistance and advice provided by a company to those people who buy or use its products or services.*"

As I see it, offering assistance and advice must include dealing with a customer's problem. Do you agree?

## What if it's Your Problem?

During a trip to Germany in the summer of 2017, my wife and I stayed in a small community called Bad Säckingen, a rural town located in the very southwest of Germany next to the Swiss border, on the Rhine River. My wife was conducting business there with her global colleagues. One of our group members was having difficulty accessing euros through a few of the local bank machines. They asked a local merchant if they could assist them and the response was, "*No, that's your problem.*" Wow! What a contrast to the above-noted restaurant story. The key for me is that even if you can't 'help', can you at least suggest or direct me to someone who can? It seems so simple and it's the right thing to do!

When was the last time that you experienced Remarkable Service? Ideally, it is good and above-and-beyond, but it doesn't have to be big.

As you are out and about today, see if you can observe Remarkable Service. If you are working in your place of business, try to deliver Remarkable Service and make your customer's problem your problem. They will love you for it.

# Jets Break Sound Barriers, Not Guitars

In 2008 Dave Carroll was headed from Halifax to Nebraska to perform with his band. His bags and guitars were packed and they were set to go. The trip proved to be Remarkable, in fact so Remarkable that over 17.5 million viewers learned of his story on YouTube – 'United Breaks Guitars'. Check it out!

I had the good fortune to meet and hear Dave's presentation and he was gracious to provide me time to interview him over a phone call and he shared his side of the story, 'United Breaks Guitars'.

On March 31, 2008, I was traveling with my brother Don and a couple other musicians. Our band was called Sons of Maxwell and we were going to Nebraska for six shows. We boarded a United Airlines flight here in Halifax. It was the first time I'd actually ever flown on United, and we flew to Omaha by way of Chicago. When we got to Chicago to de-plane and catch our connector, there was a passenger on the plane who was looking outside and declared "*they're throwing guitars outside.*" It turns out that my Taylor guitar, (everyone in the band had a guitar with them) was pretty badly damaged and I didn't find out about it though until sound check when we got to Nebraska the next morning. So, I tried to get the airline to take responsibility for it a few days later on my way back, knowing that they would not just take a phone call and send me a cheque. They'd have to triage the problem.

On my return flight home in Omaha the person to whom I tried to show the guitar said it "wasn't their responsibility" and that I'd have to "take it back to the city I started from", which was Halifax.

The reason I think that is important is because one of the problems later on down the line was they said I didn't open up a claim within 24 hours when that same person, if I had shown them right out of my guitar case, they probably would've said I have to go back to where I started out at and it wasn't their responsibility. It was, I guess, just an example of the lack of continuity within the organization. I got back to Halifax and called 1 800 numbers and wasn't getting any help. The 1 800 number took me directly to India and the people there were really great, they seemed sincerely apologetic that this thing happened, but they weren't able to take any responsibility or weren't engaged to want to. They said I had to go back to Air Canada at the Halifax airport because United doesn't really have an official presence there. Air Canada took a look at the guitar and acknowledged that it was broken, but said they were going to give me a claim number but deny it on their behalf and I would have to settle with United, which kind of made sense. That's how it kind of all started.

Nine months later I was calling all the numbers every now and again. Every week or two I would call back and eventually I heard from a customer service rep named Ms. Irlwig. She was a customer service person from Chicago and we were communicating by email and it's at that point, after all those months that she said that they weren't responsible for the damage to the guitar because I didn't open up a claim within 24 hours. At that point, as frustrated as you can imagine I was, I typed back to her in real-time that if I were a lawyer, I would sue United, but instead I was going to do something else. My something else involved making music videos and I would create three songs to make three music videos that I would post on YouTube with the goal of getting 1 million hits in the next year with all three videos combined.

I just chose three and I don't know why I chose three, but I did, and I chose a million  because it seemed like a big number. I said that I would be doing that and that I would keep her up-to-date on the progress of the project, so that when I was ready I could reach out to her and she could watch it, and together, we'd get to a million that much quicker – those were my parting words to Ms. Irlwig. That was in December of 2008 and in January I started on the project. Because it wasn't my main priority and I didn't have the money to make three songs, record them and make three videos, I wasn't sure how I was going to do it, but I had to make one song at the time which is the only way that you can do anything in life.

I wrote the first song and I instantly felt empowered and that I'd taken my power back and I stopped being angry. The song was funny and the ideas I was having were really lightening the mood and I finished what I thought was a good song in a day. I made a demo of it and sent it to my friends in the music business who all agreed that it was a tragedy what happened and they would help make a free recording. So, I had the recording done and it was really professional sounding. Then I took that recording and sent it to my friends in the film business here in Halifax who agreed to give me a one-day video shoot at no cost. They had a really small crew of three or four people and I would have to go source the actors and arrange all of the logistical aspects of the day like props, locations and lunch. I spent a lot of time doing things with no experience and making props that I'm not really great at, but I had a lot of fun doing that. We all met at the Waverley Fire Hall, just up the street from where I was living here in Halifax and where I was a volunteer firefighter at the time. The chief allowed us to shoot what ended up looking like an airport tarmac scene and all the outdoor scenes in the video are at the Waverly Fire Hall in June of 2009. The day came and went and I felt really good about what we'd done and again, really empowered by the process of bringing friends together and laughing all day about this thing. When I finally got the video, it was on Canada Day and I was really impressed with the quality that Lara Cassidy, as the Director, had cut and made a really good-looking video. It exceeded what I expected and so I hoped for the best. A week later, I still hadn't done anything to promote it because I had ambitions of creating a social media strategy to promote it, so I simply posted it on YouTube on Monday July 6th at 11:30 PM. That became my social media strategy for United Breaks Guitars and 30 Minutes later I had 6 hits. I thought all six were mine because at the time, social media was new to everybody, especially me, and so I didn't know that if you watched a video a thousand times from your house that it would only count as one. What I had done was post it to YouTube and then I sent out two messages; one to everybody on Facebook and one to everybody in my email outlook express database which was about 400 and 300 respectively. I sent one message in each direction saying United broke my guitar, can you watch this and basically, that's the last time I ever asked anybody to watch it. What ended up happening is 'United Breaks Guitar' became this truly organic viral video. A media frenzy started the next day with the LA Times being the first major media source to share the story and things really picked up. By Friday of that week I had reached my goal of 1 million views. It reached 2 million by Sunday and 3 million the following week. I had this really quick spike and then a continual slow upgrade to get to several million before the end of the summer. It turned into a media frenzy where I guess it really touched a nerve because everybody in the world has had an airline issue and United has offered enough poor experiences that they may be the airline people love to hate. People were sharing it like wildfire and I found out later that people were listening to 'United Breaks Guitar', being entertained by it and telling their friends and then they'd go to work around the water cooler and say Hey, have you seen the video by this guy, David Carroll, and then it would spark maybe two hours of bad customer service stories that people would just sort of share with each other. It became a real coming together piece.

**In September, 2009, The Economist and BBC news reported that my video was responsible for a 10% market cap drop in United Stock, or $180 million**, but it was also at the centre of other honours in the media. It was in Time Magazine's Top 10 Viral videos of the year and the BBC Radio's Internet Song of the Year. It was also a Jeopardy question, and a thousand dollar one, no less. I was getting emails from consumers all over the world that were really empowering, from people that were having a hard time putting together English sentences, saying congratulations for doing something good for customers; I have the same problem. It really reminded me how connected we all are as human beings and how so many of us share the sense of being disrespected as customers.

Then I also heard from the pilots and the flight attendants from United on their own letterheads basically saying they were sorry for what happened. That's when I started joining/connecting the dots between bad customer service and the climate inside an organization and their culture. Not long after the video went viral, I got asked to my very first speaking event and I'd never done any, but it was something I thought I could really do well if I applied myself. Because I'd been on stage many times and I like engaging with audiences through music and the telling of stories through songs, I thought I could develop a skill for speaking as well. I discovered I really liked it and for the past 7 years I've been devoting my time building a speaking career in the areas of customer experience, branding, storytelling and why our connection with one another can be the foundation of a "compassionately designed" business where you care for all stakeholders simultaneously; where customer delight and employee engagement matter as much as profit and shareholder value. Your organization doesn't have to subscribe to a war room culture of one winner and many losers. That video really did transform my life. I went from being a 20 year independent singer-songwriter, making my music and making that my soul occupation, to now, being thrust onto a platform. I was given a gift of being able to advocate for other people and as a businessman see both sides. I'm not just a consumer advocate who thinks that all businesses are evil. For the time being at least, we all need to work and earn money to live in this world but companies can strive for a balanced approach with regards to stakeholders in creating their corporate culture. I believe the right path is through the encouragement of compassion as a core value and finding pain points in your organization to alleviate them.

I have told this story a lot but I really never get tired of it because I really do know that I didn't just create this thing by myself out of nowhere. It was a communal effort. It was the friends who donated their talent and time to make the recording and the video. It was the millions of people who took the time to watch and share the video. It was a rare, organic coming-together-moment from the outset. That's what makes it all so special to me. Every time I tell it I get to re-experience the gratitude and I feel the love for the story from my audiences. I'm a lucky guy.

Dave Carroll wasn't the first person abused by an airline's customer service. But he was the first to show how one person, armed with creativity, some friends, $150, and the Internet, could turn an entire industry upside down.

At the time of writing this revised edition of my book, the story about United Airlines personnel dragging a passenger off a flight hit the news in April 2017.

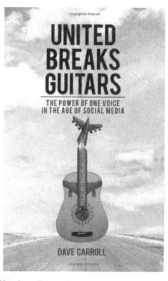

Dave Carroll was interviewed on many networks as that United Airlines incident brought back many memories. His 2009 YouTube hit actually had an increase in views of over a half-million in the first week after the United Airlines story of April 2017 broke. This incident impacted United Airlines with tons of negative press and angry passengers, not to mention a big impact on the stock value, which purportedly dropped over $700 million within a week after the story hit the news.

Bad customer service can really hit your bottom-line hard. Whether you are a billion-dollar company or a small shop, think twice when you negatively impact your customer. This is particularly important since smartphones and videos are a click away from broadcasting globally in minutes.

# Mistakes to Avoid

There are a several mistakes companies make which contribute to poor or unremarkable service. In fact, it's a bit ironic that a lot of businesses feel that they provide great customer service, but the reason they feel that way is because they don't ever ask their customers about your thoughts and views on the overall level of service.

Key mistakes to avoid:

1.  They don't take the time to have a proper mechanism to get valuable, concrete feedback on customer service. Did they ask if their customers were happy with their service and how it could be improved? E.g. What is one thing that our business can improve upon to provide you with better service? Some organizations may use The Net Promoter Score which is an index ranging from -100 to 100 that measures the willingness of customers to recommend a company's products or services to others. It is used as a proxy for gauging the customer's overall satisfaction with a company's product or service and the customer's loyalty to the brand.

2.  They turn a blind eye on customer service issues that occur in their business. Find out if it is an isolated situation. Get on top

of it, and ideally ensure that it doesn't happen again. Who was responsible and accountable for the service issue? Meet with them and find out more information and correct the problem from happening again.

3. They don't track the status of problems and resolve customer service issues. When customer service issues occur, and they will, you must ensure that things don't fall through the cracks. When did we say that we would get back to the customer? Who committed what to the customer? These are all key aspects to resolve a customer service problem.

4. We don't inspect what we expect with our employees. Perhaps a new employee was instructed to do something to support a customer. Did you follow-up (i.e. inspect) to make sure that it was done? You don't have to do this forever, but you must first trust that it is going to get done and that you have processes in place to consistently get it done.

5. There is a lack of defined role clarity. Who should do 'what' when it comes to customer service, and particularly when resolving an issue? Too often, we hear things like, "*That wasn't my job; I thought it was yours,*" or, "*I assumed you were going to do that.*" Take the time to define

functional roles and the associated duties and tasks that go with those roles.

6. They abuse their customers and treat them with disrespect. No business will ever win the day if they do this to a customer. Always think Win-Win!

7. Never assume that all of your employees are doing everything exactly the way that they are supposed to. On-the-job training and coaching is key and considered a must. Observe what they are doing and how they are doing it. (Constant and never-ending improvement is key when it comes to Customer Service.)

8. Don't compare your business to your competition. Average businesses compare themselves to other businesses and that is why they are average. You must compare your current level of performance and overall Customer Service to your desired potential. You must know what your competitors are doing, but focus on creating the best in class service culture possible for your business.

# Remarkably Good vs. Remarkably Bad

There can be a subtle difference, but when you see it, you will know. I have a keen eye to see the difference, simply because it is part of our business to see the difference. Like a musician that can hear a note played off key, I pay close attention when service is delivered on key (i.e. Remarkably Good) and when it is off the mark (i.e. Remarkably Bad).

I like to use sports analogies from time-to-time to bring home a point. When I noted that there is a subtle difference between Remarkably Good Service and Remarkably Bad Service, it is like losing a one-goal hockey game. It hurts when that happens (our Edmonton Oilers hockey team know this well), but what if it happens way too often? What one or two tweaks to the 'game-plan' could have made the difference? Could we have paid more attention to detail? Was it about the 'little things' that were missed or forgotten?

## Flying High Doesn't Make Me Want to Smile

As some of you may recall, back in 2000, two major Canadian airlines merged after an acquisition. It was a stressful time for their employees as there was a lot of eventual job redundancy. Some much needed 'post-merger integration' was required to align this business. Customers/passengers didn't receive a lot of Remarkable Service back then, as I recall. I remember this time very well as I travelled regularly from Edmonton to Toronto every other week for months to meet with my boss and other colleagues across the country for regular planning meetings. On one trip, a former colleague and long-time friend, Al Mactier, was travelling from Victoria, British Columbia to Toronto. He approached the ticket counter to check his baggage. Al noticed the airline representative struggling/arguing with a customer, and when they finished, it was now Al's turn to be served. He could tell she was upset and was totally stressed out with her day. Al is great with customers and always has a big smile, so he looked at the airline representative and said to her, with a grin ☺, "*You know, it may help if you smiled at your customers.*"

Her reply was fast and direct. "*SIR, if you had my job, you wouldn't smile either.*"

Al wittily replied, "*You may want to think about getting a different job.*"

Hopefully she found her smile again in a new/different job after the merger.

In today's world, most consumers and businesses are connected in some way to Social Media. Whether it is LinkedIn, Twitter, Facebook, or YouTube (like Dave Carroll and his United Airlines video), it is easy to get the word out there. What is the word, exactly? Well, it can be something great about your business or something negative or concerning regarding your business. What businesses need to know is that regardless of their business being active users of Social Media, others can still comment about your business. What are they saying? It could be a delightful post about how *remarkably* the business delivered service, or it could be how a customer interaction went wrong and a disagreement occurred. In today's world, it's easy for a dissatisfied customer to turn on the video on their smartphone and start rolling. In minutes, it can be spread across the globe.

I remember a story that a business owner told me a few years back about their business. A situation occurred where a customer was extremely upset about a poor service experience. The customer was quite irritated and didn't even wait three minutes after the dialogue with the business ended, to post an ugly comment on Facebook. The reality was that the story was blown out of proportion, but that didn't matter. The damage was done! The comments spread quickly, and there were 20 or 30 comments from other customers who wanted more details on exactly what took place. Fortunately, the business owner was quick thinking and called the customer who created the original post and was able to diffuse the situation and the customer agreed to send a follow-up comment to suggest that he overreacted. Wow! You see how quickly this can happen. In the blink of an eye or the click of a **mouse**, bad and concerning news can be spread about your business in seconds. Be careful out there!!

**Customer Service**

A 'bad' business experience could be a one-off, or more importantly, could easily be my business or your business, if we happened to underwhelm a customer at any given time. We need to remember that good and bad service is all about perception and we can be on the bad end of a story in the blink of an eye. Let's do our part to keep stories about our business *Remarkably* great!

# Service Tales from Germany

In July 2017, my wife Bonita and I took a trip to Germany. It was a business trip for Bonita but I was happy to be able to join her and just be a tourist. While she was busy with business meetings, I decided to hop on a train and head to Munich. It was my first time there and what an amazing city! Bonita likes to do all the research for hotels and she had picked out an amazing hotel near Olympic Park (the park was constructed for the 1972 Summer Olympics). The hotel was also near BMW Welt and the museum, which I was going to tour during my stay in Munich (I love the BMW brand and their product!). The hotel she selected was

Leonardo Hotel Munich City Olympiapark, which seemed perfect. When I arrived after my 4-hour train ride through southern Germany, I could see that it was a beautifully appointed hotel with very friendly staff that could speak English really well. This was a huge plus as my German is virtually non-existent.

The check-in was easy and quick and I smiled as I entered my room because I was so impressed with how quaint and tidy it was. The air conditioner was an added bonus as it was an especially hot day in Munich.

As it was close to dinnertime when I checked in, I was getting hungry and decided I wanted some authentic German food. I went down to the front desk and asked the lovely and extremely friendly attendant who spoke great English what she would recommend for a restaurant. She of course, suggested the hotel restaurant would serve my needs but I explained I was looking for a more authentic experience where I could sit out on a patio and enjoy a great German beer and some tasty German food. She recommended Neuhauser Augustiner, which was about a five- minute walk and I was happy to give my legs a stretch. The dinner and service were excellent. When I arrived back it was still early and I went for a nice long stroll through the local park to check out the beautiful views of Munich and they were indeed impressive. When I got back to the hotel, I noticed a bunch of people sitting outside at tables near the front side of the hotel. It was such a gorgeous evening,

I decided to order a beer and soak up a bit more of the Munich culture.

As I was outside, I wasn't sure what to expect for service, but to my delight, it was quick and courteous, and of course the beer was incredibly tasty!

As I was heading to BMW Welt the next morning, I had asked the front desk if they could book me a taxi. When I left the hotel to catch my taxi, there were so many people getting taxis that I realized I had actually missed mine. When the next taxi showed up, the driver wouldn't let me in as he had to confirm who had ordered the car. I told him that someone else had grabbed my taxi, but he was having none of it and went inside the hotel to confirm, so in I went with him. The hotel front desk attendant was awesome and said, "*This car is for Mr. Mack*" and then she literally walked me out to the taxi to make sure I got into the car. What started out as an annoyance was quickly and efficiently remedied.

The Leonardo Hotel Munich City Olympiapark is a hidden gem and I would highly recommend it. I gave them an excellent review on Trip Advisor and if I were travelling around Europe, I wouldn't hesitate to book one of their many properties. As part of the journey in writing this book, I decided to reach out and contact the hotel and thank them for their service. I spoke to the Operations Manager over a phone call from Canada at the hotel and complimented him on how amazing their service was. He was grateful for my kind words and provided a few comments about how they feel focus on customer service, which I've noted below. A big thanks to Alessandro Casola for his time and efforts.

*Dear Mike,*

*"For us it is very important to look at our Hotel with guest's eyes to detect areas of improvement and to reach our ultimate goal: guest satisfaction. Remarkable Customer Service is a main part of our business, because it makes the difference in times of growing competition and transparency. For that reason it is very important that our employees love their work, since guests notice, if they don't. I am looking forward to hearing from you and seeing you again."*

*Best regards,*

*Alessandro Casola| Operations Manager*
*Leonardo Hotel Munich City Olympiapark*
*www.leonardo-hotels.com*

# You Had Me at Coke and Chips

Ron Tite is a marketing guru based in Toronto (Founder of TheTiteGroup.com) and an amazing keynote speaker. I have had the good fortune of meeting Ron twice and have built a friendship with him. It was easy as Ron is such an awesome and friendly guy. Ron travels a ton, and one of his trips to Vancouver was so Remarkable that I asked him if I could interview him and use his story in my book. Ron agreed, and here is his Remarkable Customer Service story.

I'll give you a bit of context. I'm in Vancouver probably 12 times a year and typically for ease and simplicity, I just stay wherever the gig is. The first time I stayed at the Westin Grand was because I was booked around the corner at the Center for the Performing Arts and that was close to the hotel. It just started innocently enough, I started there and I really liked the hotel. It's nothing too fancy, it's convenient, it's close, the service is great and it's not pretentious in anyway. It's not like service in the way that sometimes people like to describe service, where it's really, really over-the-top, it's just completely friendly, completely accessible and they just take care of everything. When I started to do things in the area and when I started going in more for my own work meetings, I started choosing to stay there over all the other options.

I was there once and I tweeted something out about the hotel or something about my stay and I thought Oh, I'm going to sound negative, although that wasn't what I meant it to be. I try to be a responsible tweeter and give kudos just as much as a complaint, so I just followed up that tweet with another one that said, "*By the way, I love the Westin Grand*" and within a minute the Westin Grand social media team had written back and said, "*We love you too. When are you coming to stay with us again?*" I said, "*Funny enough, I'm here now*". And they said, "*Okay, well if there's anything we can do to make your stay better, let us know.*" Now as luck would have it, that morning there was no shampoo in my room, which is not a big deal. All the ladies would say, who cares, you bring your own, but of course I'm a guy and guys don't. Guys don't care what shampoo they use typically and I certainly tell them whatever is on the counter is typically what I'm using. I don't have backup shampoo, I just use what's there and quite frankly, if there's no shampoo for one day, who gives a shit, I just use the bar of soap; it's not a big deal. I said there was no shampoo and then they wrote back, "*We're hugely apologetic, we're really sorry.*" They obviously sent somebody from the social media team to get somebody to go and replace the shampoo immediately. And so, they wrote back and said, "*The shampoo is now in your room, huge apologies.*"

I had to speak that morning and then by the time I got back to the hotel, I thought I'd just hang out in the hotel room and work from the desk. I was doing that and there was a knock at the door and there was a woman from the hotel who had a carafe of ice-water, some fresh fruit and some kind of cut up chocolate. Again, no big deal, it's not like these were really expensive items or over-the-top stuff. It was water, fruit and chocolate, that's it. But she also had a note that said:

*"Dear @Ron Tite, thank you for being a loyal guest and follower. We hope you enjoy the rest of your stay and a little treat from us. Sincerely, @The Westin Grand.'*

So, a couple things stood out there; one, the fact that they were able to mobilize the social media team who's

somewhere in the building with something with the food prepared in the kitchen, delivered by somebody who I'm assuming is not the social media team, somebody from the hotel staff and the fact that they were able to do it quickly. And, it was a handwritten note; it wasn't some formal thing from the general manager that was completely apologetic. It was just friendly and nice and handwritten.

I thought it was amazing that they could do all this and that the people on the street were empowered by management to be able to do this so quickly. As I started speaking, I kept talking about this as a great example of leadership, and a kind of social media integration and literally all over the world. Because in the note, they signed it, sincerely @theWestinGrand, when I was doing the speech, people would pick up on that Twitter handle and would tweet to them and say "*Hey, @TheWestinGrand... @RonTite is talking about you right now.*" Every time they were mentioned, they could see @RonTite was saying some nice things about them now.

The next time I went back to the hotel, the first thing I noticed was a note and the note said: "*Dear Ron...*", which I love, because the first note said "*Dear @RonTite*", and the second note said "*Dear Ron*", so we go from some impersonal note addressed to my Twitter feed to one that is actually addressed to me as a person. So now our relationship is becoming a little bit more comfortable and more intimate. It said, "*Dear Ron, Welcome back. It's a pleasure to have you stay with us again and we are truly grateful for the kind words you say about us during your speaking engagements. To show our appreciation, please enjoy these snacks (we hear they are your favorite) as well as a couple personal touches in your suite. Stay well @TheWestinGrand.*"

Again, a great, great note addressed in the right way. I found out later it wasn't even that they put a flag on the accounts of when is this guy coming back; they

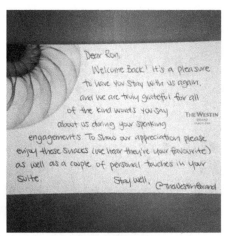

Dear Ron,

Welcome Back! It's a pleasure to have you stay with us again, and we are truly grateful for all of the kind words you say about us during your speaking engagements. To show our appreciation please enjoy these snacks (we hear they're your favourite) as well as a couple of personal touches in your Suite.

Stay well, @TheWestinGrand

THE WESTIN

actually noticed that I was speaking at an event around the corner and assumed that I was staying there and checked in and said yes, he's got a room. So that's how the social media team made that happen.

I live on Diet Coke and barbecue chips. They are two things I really enjoy. They found out about this and I found out later that they did some social media digging in terms of obviously seeing this Diet Coke addiction, but they also phoned my EA at the time and said, "*We know he really likes Diet Coke. What does he like to go along with the Diet Coke? What kind of snacks does he like?*" And so, they made that call. Now they asked my EA not to say anything about it until after the fact, because they wanted it to be a surprise. So, I see there are these two Diet Cokes in a champagne bucket, three types of homemade BBQ chips, there's one Russet potato chip, one Taro Root chip and one Kennebec potato chip.

They are all barbecue from a little chippery in Grandville Island.

They've combined this really customized, personalized experience targeted specifically at me, but also added in this air of exclusivity around it. I did not know these chips existed, I didn't know where to get these chips, would have never thought to get them, and it was such a great surprise! The next thing I went into the bathroom and there had to be 15 to 20 shampoos on the counter.

That is actually my favorite part of the whole thing. Because it's one thing to say to target customer service and surprise people, but it's something else to say we're actually more connected on a more intimate level because we can actually joke

with you and I love the personality of that. I think this is a heck of a lot more than Diet Coke, but it's fantastic!

And it also ties back this experience to the thing that they're referencing. I went into the bedroom and they had downloaded an Instagram photo of me or Facebook photo of me with our two dogs on our street outside our home. They put it in a silver frame on the bedside table with a note that says "*Hope this feels like home.*" Again, this is such an easy, easy thing to do. This isn't about budget, this isn't about strategy, this is very simply, either you have the genuine desire to make someone's day or you don't. Those people that don't make a customer's day, they have nothing but excuses. I don't have the time, I don't have the budget, I don't have the approval and all those sorts of things. I think what this whole exercise shows is that either you have a genuine desire to do it or you don't. Those people that do, will find a way. It has nothing to do with platforms, it has nothing to do with social media, it has nothing to do with having the tools at your disposal, you will just find a way.

So, I went home to my wife and showed her the photo and she said, "*If the photo was of me in the frame, I would've found that to be a little bit creepy*". This is a subject that often comes up, people say that kind of crosses the line for them where it gets a little stalkerish. Some people say that the Diet Coke, that's all great, but a photo of me; they've clearly been stalking me. I eventually met the guy who did it. I asked to meet him and be introduced to him because I wanted to interview him for a blog post. When I told him that my wife had said that that it would have been creepy, he said, "*Well actually, if we do this...,*" inferring that it is something they do a lot, which is great because you have to operationalize and scale great customer service. So, it's not the first time they did it. He said they had a policy that they will only put pictures of the people staying in the room in the frame. They won't do couple shots, they won't do anything else because you never know who's bringing who to a hotel room, which is funny. So, if I had brought somebody else to the hotel room and they see a picture of me with my wife that they didn't know existed, as immoral as that makes me as the person in that situation, still, as the customer, I am not going to be happy. Luckily, I'm not concerned about that, given my upstanding status as a husband. What I find interesting is when people say this crosses the line for me in terms of stalker behavior. I think why they made the decision to do this; to include the photo and not just the barbecue chips and the Diet Coke, was because they knew me. I have completely open profiles across every single platform, I am a completely open book, there is nothing hidden. LinkedIn, Facebook and Instagram, it's all open. So, I think if people who are in that situation, where they are all open, they're putting it all out there, they clearly don't mind if people access this, the photos and information. Those people who are maybe a little bit more closed with their social media, like my wife, who you need a password to access or you need to request her 'follow-ship', then someone like that probably isn't as into having their picture in a frame. So, it's not saying that you need to go out and ethically stalk people and do all that because that's not appropriate for every single person. The customization wasn't just in the content itself, but it was in how they presented that content that was suitable and appropriate for me. There's all these horror stories of social media where people are outed for really being an A-hole or being whatever and so I take all that away by knowing that it's a reminder for me to behave and be a great person every second of the day by making everything all good.

# Shout Out to Awesome

My business is an Authorized Partner of Everything DiSC® and The Five Behaviors of a Cohesive Team™, which are brands of the billion dollar organization, Wiley, (In existence for over 200 years). Wiley is a large corporation, but one thing is clear; they rock at what they do on every level. Their Partner Care Team is incredible and whenever we have an issue, they respond super-fast with an email or call back. It is extra special that we know all of the Partner Care Team on a first name basis. This level of personalized service and timely response is greatly appreciated, yet most of us wouldn't expect it from a giant organization like Wiley. I am grateful and honoured to be an Authorized Partner with this incredible organization and every interaction with them continues to be Remarkable.

Howard Gardiner Associates Chartered Accountants.

I have enjoyed a business relationship with the Edmonton, Alberta-based accounting firm of HGA since 2009. What makes them Remarkable is their personalized service and incredibly quick response time. While I am a small-business owner, I never feel 'small' when I need to reach out to any one of the partners, John Howard, Quentin Gardiner or Shawn Tully. Whether they are in the office or across the globe on a vacation, if I called their cell phone, I know they would

answer. This is a huge WOW for me, and a key reason that they will always have my business. They are a very progressive company and continue to expand their services, which now include accounting, legal and insurance. This is very valuable to me, as they can become my one-stop professional services provider.
**www.hgaca.com**

Just a quick bite in Zürich

On a trip to Europe, my wife and I flew into Zürich, Switzerland. We were a little bit jetlagged, but decided to tour around beautiful Zürich, which is truly an amazing city. Even though we weren't even close to adjusting to the time difference (8 hours) we had worked up a bit of an appetite on our walk. My wife, Bonita, recalled seeing a restaurant near our hotel so we didn't have to travel too far when we were done having dinner. When we got to the restaurant we quickly discovered that it wasn't open on Saturday evenings, so we went to the hotel and asked what they would recommend.

The hotel manager suggested a little Italian place about a five-minute walk down the street called Mesa. Ideally, we would have preferred traditional Swiss food for our first evening in Zürich, but the combination of jet lag and hunger made it a simple decision to try the Italian restaurant.

It was a beautiful Saturday evening but when we arrived at the restaurant there was no sign of anyone. However, the door was open so we walked in and asked if we could have a table. They stated that they wouldn't be opening until 6:30 p.m. As it was just after 6:00 p.m., we asked if it was possible for us to sit out on the patio and enjoy a nice glass of wine while we waited for them to open. The response was, "*Of course!*" We enjoyed our glass of wine immensely and the beauty and quiet of the patio. It seemed like only minutes had passed when the server came to us and said that they were ready to seat us inside. We asked if we could remain on the patio for dinner, but the server, Martin was quick to respond, "*Unfortunately no, as serving you out here would not meet our service standards. So please follow me.*"

We thought wow this is impressive! We walked in and could see that we were the first customers of the evening. They seated us at a table in the far corner, which was an intimate area where we could view the beautifully appointed restaurant, which also smelled amazing. We started by ordering two unique salads that we could taste and share. Bonita quickly commented, "*This is going to be an expensive night, considering it is a Michelin Star Restaurant.*" (The term 'Michelin Star' is a hallmark of fine dining quality, and restaurants around the world proudly promote their Michelin Star status).

I really didn't pay much attention to it because I thought, hey, this is great and we really didn't want to go anyplace else anyway.

As the food started to arrive our first few bites were amazing beyond belief. A real wow! We received great care and  attention from our server Martin, as well as from another server who didn't speak a lot of English. The host was also very attentive and stopped by to say hi. The main course arrived and it too was absolutely outstanding. Bonita and I couldn't help but comment on what a treat this was turning out to be.

During the course of the evening, the host came over to our table and we commented how impressed we were with the restaurant, the food and the service. When it was time for dessert, we had to decline, as we were just too full. I made a quick trip to the washroom because Bonita said it's a must-see, as they were immaculate, with beautifully lit candles, and heavenly scents.

I returned to our table to discover they had given us a complimentary dessert. We were grateful for the gesture and thanked the chef as he came to our table. We complimented him on the amazing experience and the absolutely delicious food and I thought, this is definitely going to go into my book.

I kindly asked the host and the chef if I could get a photo with them outside the restaurant by their sign.

By the time we left the restaurant, it was virtually full and we could tell the locals came there on a regular basis, as the host and chef were hugging and kissing many of them. Bonita and I both walked back to our hotel smiling and commenting that it was a great idea to go for "*just a quick bite*" to this gem of a restaurant. The bill was pricey, but the memory is priceless, and what a Remarkable experience for our first night in Zürich!

Tom Corley is an internationally recognized authority on habits and wealth creation.

His inspiring keynote addresses cover success habits of the rich, failure habits of the poor and  cutting edge habit change strategies.

Tom has spoken alongside *Richard Branson, Robin Sharma, Dr. Daniel Amen* and many other notable speakers.

In Tom's five-year study of the rich and poor he identified over 300 daily habits that separated the 'haves' from the 'have nots.' Tom is a bestselling and award winning author. His books include: *Rich Habits, Rich Kids* and *Change Your Habits Change Your Life* and *Rich Habits Poor Habits*.

Tom has appeared on or in *CBS Evening News, The Dave Ramsey Show, CNN, MSN Money, USA Today, the Huffington Post, Marketplace Money SUCCESS Magazine, Inc. Magazine, Money Magazine, Kiplinger's Personal Finance Magazine, Fast Company Magazine, Epoca Magazine (Brazil's largest weekly) and thousands of other media outlets in the U.S. and 25 other countries.* Tom is a frequent contributor to *Business Insider,*

*CNBC, SUCCESS Magazine* and *Credit.com.*
**www.richhabits.net**

Tom was kind enough to provide a story for my book and I am grateful for his contribution.

This is Tom's story:

In March of 2016, CNBC ran a series of articles on one of my books, Change Your Habits Change Your Life. One of those articles went viral. In less than a month, that article had over 4 million hits. Book orders surged, which was good news. The bad news was that I was, at the time, a self-published author. Because I was a self-published author, I was responsible for making sure I had enough books in inventory in order to meet the demand. With over 8,000 orders pending, I was hard pressed in finding the money to print new books in order to meet the demand. Fortunately, I was able to find the money to fulfill the orders.

Not long after the orders were filled, Hillcrest Media, my publisher, created a revolutionary new program just for me, to help me meet future demand for my books. They called it the Auto Renewal Program. Basically, they worked out a deal with their printer to fund all new book orders. Under this program, I would not have to fund future book orders – they would simply reduce my royalties by an amount equal to the printing costs for the books.

I was blown away by my publisher's desire to help me succeed as an author. That program literally changed my entire business model and the way I managed my author business. I could now focus on driving book sales without worrying about how many books I had in inventory. As a result, 2016 was my most successful year as an author and, thanks to my publisher's novel approach to solving one of my most pressing problems, 2017 is shaping up to surpass 2016.

# Customer Service Is More Than an Event

I am blessed to call Joe Ammar, President & CEO of River City Events, a dear friend and I hold him in very high regard. He is a pillar of the Edmonton community and there isn't an event in town that doesn't touch his business in some way. (Even the Mike Mack book launch in latter November 2017 was hosted by River City Events. ☺)

River City Events is a full-service event planning and rental company, providing clients with a wide array of services, including event logistics, strategic event consulting, creative event production, rentals and décor to fully support any event.

river city events
RENTALS. PLANNING. DESIGN. TENTS.

Joe Ammar founded the company in 2007, driven by a desire to create unique and memorable event experiences that build brands and relationships while celebrating special milestones.

Proudly born and raised in Edmonton, Alberta, Joe oversees all strategic and business operations for the organization. Joe's experience within the events industry spans over 30 years during which he has produced, managed and directed some of the most successful and original productions in the event industry in Edmonton and surrounding area.

Relationships are key to River City Events' ongoing success and their delivery of Remarkable Service. They take a personalized service approach that is second to none, leveraging a talented team of over 50 individuals who are empowered to achieve and develop to the next level. It is a team that is genuinely dedicated to go above and beyond to make every customer's event vision come to life.

River City Events has been blessed to work with a diverse range of clientele and have collaborated with the City of Edmonton and area on some of its most memorable events such as the Edmonton Grey Cup, Red Bull Crashed Ice, Edmonton Airshow, Edmonton Opera, Royal Alex Hospital Foundation Harvest Gala and many more.

No two days are the same in the events industry, which is exciting and challenging for River City. The company is at the forefront of events for any purpose and size and everything they do is built on delivering what the client asks for. Whether a 10,000+ person sporting event, a festival or a private function such as a wedding or gala, it's all about paying special attention to the details and ensuring they exceed their customers' expectations.

Their involvement with the most recent Edmonton Grey Cup was a Remarkable Service story, proudly remembered for its success but also as an undertaking which presented them with some exceptionally challenging event logistics. Joe notes, "Our team was planning and creating in and around a facility that was under major construction. All of our team, including our suppliers, were wearing hard hats and steel toed boots. We were all there, working together to envision what needed to be done for an event of this scale."

Commonwealth Stadium is a very large facility where timeliness, security and weather play major roles, and did it ever in this case! With a minus 30 degrees Celsius forecast on the horizon, the River City team bundled up, then huddled up, ready for a strategic install consisting of a massive inventory of tables, chairs, dishes, catering equipment and décor, all needed to create one of Edmonton's largest hospitality and sporting events. Says Joe, "We worked tirelessly to get the equipment delivered accurately and set up with reduced timelines, while obeying strict security measures in a multitude of areas all over the stadium. Imagine creating an event space overnight to host over 10,000 guests for food, bar service and entertainment and then remove it all the next day! But these events strengthen the community and build opportunity for businesses of all sizes, including ours, which we are grateful for."

Over the past 10 years, River City Events has grown by leaps and bounds, much like the City itself. The company now boasts more than 50 of the most talented and creative employees in the industry. "I am so proud of our dedicated team", says Joe. Their location in downtown Edmonton, where much of the City's recent growth and

revitalization has taken place, has also helped drive business growth. Their building, situated behind MacEwan University, and blocks from the newly built Rogers Place arena, home to the Edmonton Oilers hockey team, enables them to play a major role in creating economic growth, employment and development for new business. And despite Edmonton's fast-paced growth, Joe says the City continues to be a friendly and welcoming place where people of all backgrounds can succeed. "I truly believe Edmonton is the best place to build and create and to make something of yourself."

And he certainly has done that. Through hard work and perseverance, Joe has created a business that is not only successful, but supportive. His mindset for leading a relationship-focused organization instills energy in his people, allowing them to unleash the creative drive that produces events that wow their customers and make the team proud. Joe attributes his work ethic and mindset to an example set for him early on in life.

"I've met some incredibly smart and inspiring entrepreneurs in my life, but I have to say that some of the best business lessons I have learned were from working with my father in the grocery store he owned for nearly two decades. He taught me the importance of relationships in business, and that patience, hard work and resilience are some of the key ingredients to success."

River City Events has been recognized by numerous local organizations and associations and has been acknowledged as one of Business in Edmonton's Top 20 Leaders in 2017, Edmonton's Best Industry Professional by the Edmonton Event Awards (2017), as well as Consumer Choice Awards, and Best Designed Exhibit for five consecutive years at the Edmonton Bridal Fair.

Joe is a strong believer in giving back to the community and he supports many organizations and non-for-profit associations in our city. He is the former President of the Canadian Rental Association, Alberta Chapter, and the Honorary Chair for the 2014 Relay for Life of the Canadian Cancer Society for Strathcona County. In addition, Joe has been awarded a National Philanthropy Award from the Canadian Cancer Society in recognition of his leadership and support.

River City Events also proudly supports their clients' events through sponsorship support and the donation of thousands of dollars to many organizations including:

- Junior Achievement Awards
- Ronald McDonald House & Children's Wish Foundation
- Edmonton Chamber of Commerce
- & Many more

There is little doubt River City Events has set the bar high on delivering Remarkable Service and is well positioned for further growth, exciting new ventures and continued community involvement. They are excited to see what the future holds and grateful to grow with the city they love and serve. Learn more about River City Events: www.rivercityevents.ca

# Tim McClure's Incredible Journey

I had the privilege of listening to Tim's presentation in Alberta, Canada in June 2017 and still refer to my notes of his inspiring story and message. So many points resonated for me, including: "*If you believe in something, do it now*"; "*We think too much and feel too little*"; and "*Life is about creating memories*". Tim is a warm and passionate

people person who really made the audience sit back and reflect on our lives. I saw many teary eyes in the room and we were greatly impacted by Tim's words.

If you ever have the opportunity to hear Tim speak, I highly recommend you attend, as it will change how you think about everything in your life.

**www.timmclure.ca**

Here's Tim's story…

February 4th, 2011 is a day that will forever remain in my mind. That was the day I was diagnosed with cancer.

I remember everything like it was yesterday. The doctor asked the nurse to leave the room. I can still hear her footsteps, and the sound of the door closing behind her.

He looked at me and said, *"I'm going to give this to you straight. You have cancer. The tumor is in a delicate spot. It has spread aggressively into your lymph nodes, and it's not something that we can operate on. You're pretty far along and in Stage 4."* When I asked him how many stages there were, he looked at me and said, *"I'm sorry, there are only 4."*

How could this happen to me? Why? Will I die? How much time do I have? What about my career? How will I tell my kids? How will I be able to keep my house? Will I ever play golf again?

In just 30 seconds, my life changed forever.

Leading up to this, I was a healthy, athletic, father of 2 daughters; I traveled the world as a senior management executive, and I had more great friends than a guy could ask for... but it all seemed to come crashing down so suddenly.

Another date that will stay with me forever is May 19th, 2011. On that day, I set out to do something that none of us can ever really be prepared for. You see, on May 19th, I began to make my own funeral arrangements – I chose my pallbearers, picked the music that would be played, and I determined who would speak at my service. Pictures began to be gathered for a video that would be made and given to family and friends of us during much happier times. Certainly, it was a very difficult and daunting task.

Doctors are brilliant at what they do. Most though, are very clinical. They have to be. They see pain, suffering and death every day. It's what they do, and to do it, they must have ice in their veins. My doctors were tremendous... second to none, and they saved my life

Remember, there is the human element in all of this – the one that is so vitally important to a patient when they first receive devastating news. While my doctors were incredible, they were not the ones who were the 'wind underneath my wings'.

Among the sounds of sirens, 'Code Blue' announcements echoing through the hospital hallways, and the feeling of being locked so tightly onto the table as I slid into the machine for my daily treatments, there was someone with the name 'Tammy' on her hospital identification badge.

Bono, Madonna, Mick Jagger, Katy Perry, and Justin Bieber...these are some of the names that we think of when the word 'rock star' is used. Not me though; my rock star's name was Tammy Lui.

Tammy was a Radiation Therapist at the Sunnybrook Health Sciences Centre in Toronto, Ontario. Small in stature, and quiet by nature, she didn't really stand out when I first entered the eye of this very bad storm.

As part of my treatment plan, I would receive daily radiation treatments to support the chemotherapy that I was also receiving. Almost every day, I would interact with Tammy.

When I was first diagnosed, I was told that I should expect to lose up to 20 lbs. I unfortunately, lost 50 lbs. in just 15 weeks. I was deteriorating rapidly, becoming weaker and weaker by the day. For someone who took care of himself and went into hospital in otherwise great shape, it was devastating to my family, friends and I. It seemed that I was fading away right in front of everyone's eyes.

Needless to say, as my treatments went on, my strength was waning physically, mentally emotionally and psychologically. I really did begin to believe that the possibility of my life ending was very real.

On one particular day though, my mindset changed. It was Tammy who changed it!

Tammy had been away for a few days during my treatments on a Thursday and Friday; I would not see her again until the following Tuesday. I had been having a very rough time. I was brought into the treatment room and the first thing that she said to me was, "*Wow, you look SO much better than you did last Wednesday when I saw you.*"

My first thought was to turn around and look at whom it was that she was speaking to. Tammy went on to say, "*You have more color in your face, and you look more alert...I can see it in your eyes!*" I was floored. Here I was 50 lbs. lighter, extremely weak, my face was sunken in, and my clothes were draped over a body that consisted of skin and bones.

It was magical! She had gotten through to me; she saw something that I didn't see. Tammy had lit a spark inside of me at a time when I began to lose hope, and when I was at my darkest point. The incredible thing is, she didn't even know it!

Months later, it was deemed that I had gone into remission; I began the long road back to recovery. Worlds like 'incredible', 'amazing' and 'miracle' were being used by medical professionals.

Later that year, Sunnybrook Health Sciences Centre held the 10th Annual Schulich Award for Nursing and Clinical Excellence. I nominated Tammy and in 2011, she was named as a well-deserving recipient – just the second person from the Odette Cancer Center out of 100 winners to ever receive this prestigious award.

Tammy Lui did not only do her job well and deliver Remarkable customer care, but she played a significant role in me getting through my darkest days. The incredible thing was that until she was nominated, she didn't realize that she had made such an impact on my life. To her, she was just doing her job, and that is exactly what makes her the true professional that she has become.

Sometimes while carrying out one's professional duties, a person can make a significant impact. This gives us all proof that while saying or doing something for someone else may not change everyone's world, it certainly can change someone's world. Tammy Lui changed mine, and her impact will stay with me forever.

# A Longstanding Testament to a Remarkable Association

India-based Kapoor Lamp Shade Company's, Managing Director and CEO, Sawan Kapoor, who I have had the privilege of knowing since 2012 shared this story.

Kapoor Lamp Shade has had the good fortune of having Infosys Technologies Ltd. (The second largest IT and IT services company globally, and a well-known international business) as a customer for nearly three decades. They have provided customized lighting solutions for the majority of Infosys offices and campuses in India for over thirty years focusing on the art and science of illumination.

In 2016, Infosys Technologies Ltd. asked us to take on their first international campus project in Shanghai; a brand-new facility of over two million square feet. This would be the largest and most modern of Infosys's facilities outside of India. The campus would house fifteen thousand software engineers as well as a new facility devoted to innovation for various industries.

Other than the grand scale, there were a few things unique about this project. The first was that every other aspect and requirement of the project was being done by a Chinese company, all materials, the facility's design and the complete build was in Chinese  hands. The second was that after an internal supplier audit, and a formal RFP, Kapoor Lamps placed L2 (not the lowest priced bid), yet we were awarded the project on the basis of our exceptional score given three decades of customer service history. This project was on a very strict timeline to avail significant benefits for taxation and operation if commenced within 2016. The lights were being manufactured, bought and installed in China, however, the order was being given to us, a company from India. Infosys was so committed to having our company solely responsible for the lighting and lighting management systems, that despite resistance from the Chinese company, they publicly stood up for us and insisted that we be given this portion of the project.

Why was Kapoor Lamp Shade awarded this amazing opportunity? We believe it was because of the Remarkable relationship we had built with Infosys in almost three decades of working with them. Our ability to stay agreeable with the customer, not over-negotiate matters, and not drag the customer into the issues we would face in the process; ranked highest in their view. They had seen us demonstrate time and again that we could consistently execute large and complex projects. We had a proven track record of consistency, dependability, creativity, timely service and the highest attention to quality and details. We had always focused on elements critical to a flawless customer service and meeting and exceeding our commitment to quality. 70 years in business spanning over three generations had provided us with the knowledge and experience to deliver exceptional products and services to our customers.

Although we pride ourselves in delivering operational excellence as a leader in the lighting industry, being chosen by Infosys for the project in Shanghai reaffirmed to us the true value of providing Remarkable Service.

A Big thanks to my friend Sawan for contributing to my book. Sawan and I used to be part of an International master-mind group and I gained so many insights from him over the years. We truly live in such a small world, as he has business connections in Edmonton.

About Kapoor Lamp Shades.

Established in 1948 by Shri Om Prakash Kapoor, we are today India's oldest and most integrated lighting solutions company. What we do has touched and brightened the lives of our customers across the nation. As a one-stop lighting solutions company, today we deal in all types of lighting including decorative lighting, architectural lighting, façade lighting, outdoor and landscape lighting, as well as commercial lighting

**kapoorlamp.com/about.html**

# Five Areas That Lead to Remarkable Service

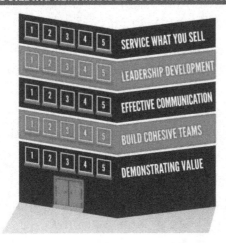

**BUILDING REMARKABLE CUSTOMER SERVICE**

1 2 3 4 5 SERVICE WHAT YOU SELL

1 2 3 4 5 LEADERSHIP DEVELOPMENT

1 2 3 4 5 EFFECTIVE COMMUNICATION

1 2 3 4 5 BUILD COHESIVE TEAMS

1 2 3 4 5 DEMONSTRATING VALUE

In my 30 plus year career, I have observed that there are five key areas that have a significant impact on building Remarkable Customer Service.

The first area is Demonstrating Value. Demonstrating value must occur before the customer cuts the cheque to your business. Demonstrating value may include your past track record and how you actually supported and assisted customers. (e.g. On-time delivery) If you have demonstrated value, you "may" earn the right to ask for testimonials, recommendations, and referrals. Demonstrating value is key and critical.

What would your customers say about the value that they receive from your business? Are they getting their monies' worth?

What demonstrating value may look like:

Offer to meet the customer or prospect when it is most convenient for them.

Provide valuable tips and insight, and don't expect to be compensated for this at the outset of the relationship.

Ask great questions before making any attempt to sell a customer/prospect on your product or service. Make it all about them.

Earn trust before earning the sale.

Offer valuable products and services that will help solve your customer's problem.

Show the benefits that your services have provided other customers.

Offer complimentary time and advice at no-cost or obligation, with no strings attached.

Be nice, and earn your customer's respect. Whether it's a phone or in-person greeting or a conflict with a customer, you have to be nice and show patience in order to earn their respect.

Rate your business in this area:

(Poor) 1---2---3---4---5 (Remarkable)

Action steps to improve your rating

_____

_____

_____


The second area is to Build Cohesive Teams. All of your employees regardless of department, must operate on the same page. Too often silos get created as one department thinks they are more valuable to the business than another department. Cohesive teams trust one another and are willing to acknowledge when they make mistakes. They are willing to have productive conflict when issues arise, but they do so to achieve a common goal for the business and for their customers. Cohesive teams are committed to what was agreed upon. There is clarity on what needs to be done and the collective team has buy-in to complete the task or project that supports customer service. They are willing to hold other team members accountable to ensure that the goal or task at hand gets completed. Ultimately, cohesive teams generate solid 'collective' results for the business.

My business is an Authorized Partner of The Five Behaviors of a Cohesive Team™.

This has been a valuable program to build a more cohesive team and help eliminate dysfunctional behaviors that may occur from time to time. Each team member completes a comprehensive assessment and provides feedback on how they view their team in terms of Trust, Conflict, Commitment, Accountability and Results. When all team members have completed the assessment, a personalized 36-page report is produced for each team member. The team will get detailed measurements on each area (i.e. Trust, Conflict, Commitment, Accountability and Results). We guide the team through structured solutions that will help reduce or eliminate any dysfunction.

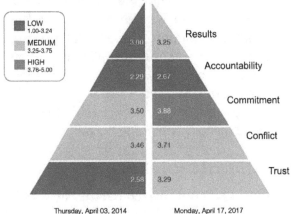

LOW
1.00-3.24

MEDIUM
3.25-3.75

HIGH
3.76-5.00

Results        3.00    3.25

Accountability   2.29    2.67

Commitment      3.50    3.88

Conflict        3.46    3.71

Trust          2.58    3.29

Thursday, April 03, 2014        Monday, April 17, 2017

Progress reports can be generated in the future (e.g. 6-12 months later) as a follow-up to determine if progress has been made to improve the overall cohesive behavior of the team.

*"We recently started to work with Mike Mack and his team and participated in the Everything DiSC Workplace® session followed by the initial stages of The Five Behaviors of a Cohesive Team ™ program. Everybody was very positive and thought it was very beneficial, and they liked the content and the process and thought that they did a very good job facilitating. Bottom-line, we thought that this was going to really help our team move forward and we are extremely positive and very encouraged by the session and what this can do for our team."*

**-Nick Parkinson**
President and CEO
**YMCA of Northern Alberta**

Is your team cohesive? Can your team be dysfunctional at times? What could be done to enhance your team's unity to keep them on the same page?

Rate your business in this area:

(Poor) 1---2---3---4---5 (Remarkable)

Action steps to improve your rating

_____

_____

_____

The third area for any business is Effective Communication with your customers and your employees when challenges arise or to simply stay connected and build trust and rapport. This seems to come up all the time. When we have an issue, we might try to avoid the issue rather than directly communicating with customers and employees of other departments, and updating them about the fact that things aren't going as we had hoped. I liken it to an airline. If we're travelling, it's nice to know if our flight has been delayed. While we may not be happy about it, it's good to know because we can change our schedules accordingly. Communicating with your customer when challenges arise is critical to business success. Communicating with your customers on a regular basis is essential to maintaining a relationship with your business. If you don't communicate, your competitors may be talking to your customers. Are you communicating regularly with your customers?

There are a number of reasons businesses don't effectively communicate with their customers when there is a challenge:

1. They are just too busy, and they don't have time. (Not a great excuse.)

2. They don't have adequate processes in place to remember to call that customer back when challenges arise. That might be relatively easy for me to do in our business, but if you're a heavy-duty truck dealership, for example, communicating with the customer may need to be assigned to someone else with the appropriate technical expertise. You have to make sure that they phone the customer back in a timely manner.

3. They are complacent: "Oh well, the customer will probably call us back anyway."

4. The lack of essential and timely information for the customer.

5. They don't like to communicate bad news. If what we're communicating to the customer may disappoint the customer that makes it a bit more difficult.

What poor communication may look like:

- Not doing what you said that you would do.

- Over promise and under deliver.

- Not returning customer calls/emails in a timely manner.

- Talking about the last customer you served in front of the current customer that you are working with. (This drives me crazy, and I see it far too often. I may be getting ready to pay for my groceries at a checkout counter, and one cashier will say something to another cashier, such as: "Wow, was that last guy ever slow.

A tip to remember when you want to effectively communicate during a customer service issue and conflict arises.

When the relationship with someone is not important and the outcome of the solution is not important, you can avoid the conflict. (e.g. a disagreement with a stranger, as it is not worth the fight)

When the relationship is important (i.e. with your customer) and the outcome of the solution is not 'as important', you can compromise (e.g. settling on the price of a low-cost repair and the difference may be a small amount of money. Is it worth losing a customer over $10, $100, or $1,000 depending on your business?)

When the relationship is VERY important (which should be the case with <u>most </u>of your customers) and the outcome of the solution is VERY important, you must "collaborate" with your customer. (You must find the win-win in the solution.)

You also have to manage your emotional intelligence and keep calm. As the old saying goes, "*The customer is always right*," and we at least have to create the perception that the customer is right because they have the <u>right</u> to voice their concerns or be unhappy with your particular service. This is a must! If you walk into a place of business and people are grumpy, rude, or defensive and don't treat you well, it will likely be a key factor in whether or not you will return to that place of business again in the future.

Never forget that "*doing what you say you're going to do*," still holds true today in business, in any industry, anywhere. Be reliable. Even if you can't deliver exactly what the customer's expectations were, be reliable enough to give them a heads-up on that. E.g. "*Your truck is not going to be ready on Friday morning, but it will be ready by late Friday afternoon*," and then honour your word at that point in time. Being reliable is critical, which is based on <u>how</u> you communicate and <u>what</u> you communicate to your customer. Be impeccable with your word! In doing so, you must always tell all of your employees exactly what was committed to your customer. If someone is missed in the process, a key step could go unnoticed and you fail to deliver on your promise. Even if only one employee makes the mistake/error, your business could be seen as unreliable in the eyes of your customer.

Rate your business in this area:

(Poor) 1---2---3---4---5 (Remarkable)

Action steps to improve your rating

_____

_____

_____

The fourth step to building Remarkable Service is Leadership Development.

*"If your actions inspire others to dream more, learn more, do more and become more, you are a leader."* -John Quincy Adams

Leadership takes focus and dedication and not everyone is cut out to be a great leader. All great leaders must create a vision that people want to follow. It can take your business and your team boldly into the future of exciting possibilities. The leader must remain open as the team may have input to enhance the direction and overall **vision.**

Great leaders work hard to build **alignment** through communication, clarity and consistent and engaging dialogue. The goal here is that the entire team is moving in the same direction. Having your team operate on the same page is key to this process. How have you demonstrated alignment with your team?

A final key step for the leader is to lead the focus on **execution** with structure and ongoing momentum, along with constant feedback to empower the team to leverage its talents and strive to realize their vision. Without execution, your vision can never be realized!

*"Even in an organization that's doing something big and bold, there's the mundane, day-to-day execution work of keeping it going. But people need to stay connected to the boldness, to the vision, and stay plugged in to the main vein of the dream."* -Peter Diamandis

Note: The Work of Leaders report is affiliated with my Authorized Partnership with Wiley. (Ask for me for the 23-page "sample report" if you wish to learn more.)

Leadership Development includes strong coaching skills. Coaching is not commonplace in many organizations. It is rare to see a leader spending one-on-one time with a team member that may be struggling. I attribute this to the time and overall skills needed to be an effective coach. Some see it as warm and fuzzy and not productive. Great coaching does enhance the overall performance of your team. It's a must!

There is also a big difference between leading and managing. You must lead people and manage things. Not every leader or manager gets this.

Leaders must create opportunities for growth as most employees crave this. Training and ongoing coaching support are critical to your organization's overall success.

Rate your business as it relates to Leadership:

(Poor) 1---2---3---4---5 (Remarkable)

Action steps to improve your rating

_____

_____

_____

The final step to building Remarkable Customer Service is to always Service what you Sell. When was the last time that you looked at all aspects of your business from the perspective of your customers? This may not be a common practice that most business owners or leaders do. Some businesses do a good job of structured customer surveys that offer tangible feedback, but many don't have a process in place to obtain feedback. (e.g. The Net Promoter Score, which was referenced in the 'Mistakes to Avoid' chapter earlier in the book).

Let's use a car dealership as an example. Buying a new car is usually an exciting, and for the most part, an enjoyable experience. But, when we take that new vehicle in for a service appointment, it can be a very different experience. You may become a transaction and the love is gone. Sales, Service and Parts, must play on the same team and make the 'customer' experience a pleasant one. I heard this line many years ago from a seasoned automotive sales professional. He said, *"The sales team sells the first vehicle, but 'service' will sell the next one.*" How true!! Customers tend to have long memories, especially when they have experienced crappy service. It becomes very difficult to sell the customer on a new vehicle, or product, when you have a file of bad service memories that you had to deal with. This concept holds true in any industry, whether you are a hotel, accounting firm or dress shop. Service matters in sales. It always has and it always will.

Business leaders often ask me, "How do we increase sales?" While there are many fundamental activities that need to occur (i.e. weekly/monthly planning, focus on the ideal/target customer for your products and services, soft skills of the sales team, etc.), customer service within your business must be 'consistent and good.' Most customers will tolerate a mistake now and then, as long as your business acknowledges the mistake. If your service isn't great and there are too many examples of customer issues and complaints, it will be hard to make another sale to the dissatisfied customer. Being a great sales person can't win the day when a customer has unresolved service issues, or a laundry list of bad service experiences at your business.

What Sales without Service looks like.

- Making it more about you than the customer.

- Being inflexible to customer requirements.

- Over-selling and avoiding truly listening and understanding what the customer/prospect wants.

- Over promising and under delivering, just to keep the customer from complaining more.

Rate your business in this area:

(Poor) 1---2---3---4---5 (Remarkable)

Action steps to improve your rating

_____

_____

_____

# Making IT Remarkable!

I have heard many amazing stories about CompuVision, **www.compuvision.biz** but I hadn't had the pleasure of meeting their CEO, Ryan Vestby. In early summer 2017, Ryan and I chatted at the 55 North conference in Grande Prairie, Alberta. Ryan was kind enough to offer a follow-up visit to get to know each other better. I was grateful to connect with Ryan in August 2017 over lunch and receive a tour of their Head Office in Edmonton, Alberta. I was so impressed with Ryan's leadership and what his team was doing from a customer service perspective, that I asked if Ryan would allow some  extra time for an interview so that I could capture his words in my book.

Here is the interview and some Remarkable insight from Ryan.

Why is it so important that in regards to engaging a prospective customer, you do what you do and why have you designed your model the way you have?

Ryan: This really came about by 'not racing to the bottom in regard to pricing'. The challenge we've seen in a lot of different verticals, especially our vertical, is that people just seem to be chasing each other to the bottom in regard to pricing. So, they are going to win on price every time on RFP's when they are bidding against somebody. Every time you take away a dollar margin or you take away some of that price point, it takes away some of the ingredients that go into your recipe. We talk a lot about a recipe here and it's kind of our philosophy that we believe that we have an unbelievable recipe that can only be delivered with a certain amount of ingredients in the right order, in the right fashion, which in turn, will deliver a predictable result. We talk a lot about ourselves internally, we jokingly call ourselves bakers and we have created a tasty chocolate cake recipe. We know that we can repeat it every time with the right ingredients at the right time and when everything is lined up we can reproduce this. The problem is, if all of a sudden, your customers are forcing you to buy your ingredients from other places, it becomes very difficult. Or if they don't value a particular ingredient in your recipe, then they don't want to buy it. The challenge with that is if they start taking apart what the recipe is, you've just become diminished to a grocer. Now anyone can buy all the ingredients and hopefully, the result turns out to what the baker can bake. Everything stemmed from that and so probably three years ago we said to ourselves, we don't want to be a low-cost provider. We want to deliver a service that we know is going to change the way people view IT. It's going to drive efficiencies to their business through what we do and how we do it and we removed any KPI's of growth. We truly said, "You know what, if we don't sign up another customer this year, that's ok, as long as we only sign up customers that fit what we value." We looked at our entire book of business and we let about 12% of it go. Either they didn't value us, they wanted a low-cost solution, they never did any recommendations or never did anything that we told them to do. They were just using us as a kind of an insurance policy. When the mindset changed, everything started to happen for us. If you take away the KPI (Key Performance Indicator) of not worrying about new sales and only worry about protecting the house and taking care of the customers that value what you do and value your chocolate cake recipe, good things happen. What we found is our customer satisfaction went up and our employee satisfaction went up because now they were only dealing with organizations that really valued what they did to help them. Profitability went up because we weren't chasing low dollars. All those things started to happen and it became the self-fulfilling prophecy where now the by-product of sticking true to those thoughts was making more money and having happier customers and happier employees. That was really how this all started for us and then the emotional aspect for us, where it came in to play, was we are probably the most expensive managed service provider in western Canada, if not Canada for sure. A big portion of that is for us to deliver the recipe we want to deliver; you need to have all these ingredients in place. But you can't articulate that or show that with a pricing sheet, or a proposal, or a website. So, we shifted gears a year ago and decided to revamp our website. I really didn't want anything on there, basically our call to action is that you come to our office for a tour and that's it. That's completely different from anybody else in our marketplace. If I pulled up my top 10 competitors in Edmonton or western Canada, their websites would look exactly the same. They'd have an intro video of what their services are about, they might have some pricing, they might have all the things that are included and almost look the same. You could literally just interchange their logos and colors and it would be the same website. For me, we wanted a true emotional response to what we do, because when shit is going south in a business and when there's chaos in regard to the IT infrastructure side of things, people really feel it. It's an emotional pain point for them and so that's what we wanted to capture when people came to our website. They come there and literally, there's a crazy storm that has nothing to do with IT but has everything to do with emotions and how you feel about it and the call to action is, you just have to come for an office tour. The biggest reason why we do that is because we need to control the narrative of why we're the most expensive but it's the best money they'll ever spend. That's really where the magic happens for us. Once we get them in the door, they invest the time, they're intrigued enough or their interest is tweaked enough to say *"I've got to learn more, this is unlike anything I've experienced so far from a sales process."* That's where really the customization of the personalization came to play. This has been my vision for probably 3 to 4 years: to customize, almost like a skin or a layer to whoever is coming through our doors, be it a prospect, be it an interviewer, be it a supplier, that we could just change the office in a heartbeat to match who was coming through the door. We do that where we change the colors of the walls, we put custom logos and names on the walls, we have a projection mapping which we pull videos and imagery from people's websites and it just gives  this personalized feel, but more importantly, the tour that we give is almost identical for everybody.

Internally, I always say this is like a Broadway play. We all work here and we manage technology and we manage people's infrastructure and their problems, but we're part of a bigger narrative, part of a bigger kind of initiative and this is like a Broadway play. It's going to be the same set every time, we're going to walk through it the same way, we are going to explain every screen, every aspect, every HR component the same way. That way, there's consistency of the conversation that we're delivering to these people. What blows my mind, even to this day, we've probably done over 50+ tours so far over the last 3 to 4 months and almost every tour, people bring out their cameras to take photos of the personalization because it gives them ideas. If we look at what we do as an organization, we want to be that technology connector, we want to be able to inject ideas and help them ethically disrupt their business in whichever way we can. I want to be that idea factory. I want to be the place that they go, *"Gosh! Can I take a picture of this? We've got to do this! We could do this on our welcome wall. We can do this in our business."*

If it all stems from these ideas coming from us and being generated through the tour and what we're doing to personalize it, that just leaves marks on people in regard to something that is memorable. If you think about how many interactions and data that we come across today, there's so much noise out there and what do we truly remember? What is it that truly impacts us? I just think about the noise that is generated on social media and all these feeds we have of data, there is nothing that really sticks. It's all just white noise. The personalization part and having somebody that you have a narrative with and really connecting with all the attention to detail, becomes really powerful. As I say to my staff, "*we are planting a seed in them today; they might not buy today, but that's alright. No matter where they go to buy a service similar to ours, they are always going to remember this and now the bar is set.*" They're not going to get the same experience if they go to a low-cost provider. And every time there is a pain, they are going to recall, "*Gosh do you remember that company that we toured? They seemed to have everything going on, their personalized attention to detail, they took imagery from our website and really took the time to learn who we are.*" That seed is in them and it's just going to grow. Other people's pain is really where our value is going to come in. We found that our close ratio is incredibly high when we tour people through the office.

How does this strategy work for potential clients that aren't local? How do you 'plant the seed', as you say, for a business across the country?

Ryan: We want to be known as a technology connection company and what better way than to leverage technology itself to tour people. We have a full VR tour that is available online that is the same narrative, the same Broadway play that we do as if you're standing here with us. People can click on the virtual tour and we overnight them custom Google cardboard VR goggles. They show up at their office the next day, they basically put their phone in these VR goggles and they get to experience the full tour of our office. You may think it might not be as good as actually being there, but sometimes it's better because we have the ability to show them a new piece of technology that they're probably not even aware of, let alone used before and we're the ones that introduced it to them simultaneously through a connection or a button on a website. Those Google cardboard CompuVision branded goggles are now in the homes of our prospects. They are going to show them to their kids and their wife and their executive teams and all those things are going to happen and it's just another seed that's been planted. They'll be going "*Gosh those guys are really with it and they're really up on technology*." The one thing I tell all my staff is, at the end of the day, I want that prospective customer to walk out the door and say to themselves "*If we want technology in our business, in our roofing company or our accounting firm or our manufacturing organization, we've got to work with these guys!*" That is where everything stemmed from.

What are some of the results or perhaps comments that your customers would share?

Ryan: I think that when someone has come from a prospect all the way to the finish line to being a customer and they've experienced this personalization or us opening our doors to show them not only what our service is, but how we are as human beings or how we are as community partners or how we treat our employees and what we focus on. I think that is as much of what they're buying as our service. They want to be aligned with that, they want their company to do the same thing, they want to treat their people and what they focus on similarly. There is alignment there. I find when people have gone through the whole process to get across the finish line, it's almost like somebody has opened up their home. There is nothing more intimate than a family dinner and for us to open up our place of work and share it at such an intimate level of what we do and how we deal with our people and how everyone's pictures and bios are on the wall. We share what we do culturally, all those things become really important to say yes, there is an alignment and I see where our company is going. We are aligning more with companies that have similar cultures. I don't want to deal with customers that treat their employees like shit or treat their clients like shit. I just don't want to deal with those people. I'll quote one of my good friends, Ryan Pomeroy, "*I only want to do business with people that I like, people that I'm willing to go to dinner with.*" If you aren't willing to go for dinner with every one of your customers, then you probably have the wrong customers. If you aren't going to invite them for family dinner to meet your family or sit down and break bread for 2 or 3 hours, are those the people you want to be spending time with? What really resonates and sticks with our customers is understanding that, really looking under the hood of what we do and how we do it and how we treat them.

One of our real key initiatives that has been super successful to separate the transactional type of work we do for our customers is to really focus on the humanized aspect of it. We have this program, called the **WoWance Program** that is really geared towards identifying events in people's lives as we are dealing with their fires when they call us. We're dealing on a day-to-day basis with people that are having problems in their infrastructure in regard to troubleshooting Excel, to their networks, to their servers. Through that, you have lots of conversations with people and they open up about their real-life problems and issues that they're dealing with. All our people are trained to identify them and write them down and to listen for those cues that are sometimes just so subliminal that you wouldn't recognize them if you weren't listening. It could be that someone's dog died, their daughter is getting married, they just bought a new car or someone just graduated. Whatever that is, we identify it. We, as an organization, promote all our people to write something personal and send them a small gift. We cover all the costs and all they need to do is execute and send it to one of our admin staff and say "*Hey, I want to write this note and send this bouquet of flowers or these cookies or whatever to this customer.*" This now builds this goodwill in the tank that is on this human level, that has nothing to do with the IT support that they got, but has everything to do with the conversation that they had of real life. I'll tell you right now, you can reach people on a human level by sending them an edible arrangement because their dog passed and you understand because you have a dog or you send out a celebratory basket of cookies because their firstborn just graduated from high school. I don't know too many suppliers, let alone any IT company that are taking the time to do that. It's these kinds of things - if we start driving every action from the kind of root cause of being human beings, man oh man, can you really get some traction with people.

As a final question, what do you hope that your prospects and customers are remarking about specific to your business today?

Ryan: It's not about the transactional services that we provide, we do hundreds and hundreds of tickets a day for 10,000 assets across the country and those just happen. You have to be good at those. The thing that would basically check the box for me that we're doing everything right, would be that our customers are looking at us from a Remarkable perspective and saying, "*These people are truly trying to change our business for the better. They are helping us retool our industry, our business to help us to ethically disrupt ourselves so that we're prepared that no one else is going to disrupt us.*" I just think a lot of organizations hear the buzzwords of *innovation* and *disruption.* As you mentioned earlier, it's really prevalent right now, but they have no idea how to go about doing that. If you think about disruption, it's coming from technology, it's coming from innovation and these are not companies that traditionally are connected with innovation and technology. They're a roofing company, they're a manufacturing company, they're a golf course, they're an accounting firm, they are not technology firms. Everyone needs to reframe their view on their own business and they need to reframe it saying they're a technology company that does accounting, they're a technology company that runs a golf course and if they do that, that is where they're going to survive in the future. For me, it's about helping them get there. Our tagline is: *Changing the Way You Do Business.* It couldn't be any clearer. If I can help them change the way they do roofing or help them change the way they handle accounting through technology and innovation and disruption, I don't know what would check the box deeper than that. I believe they will pay all day long for our technical services when we've helped them at such a higher level change their entire business by injecting this technology.

A big thank you to Ryan for taking the time and allowing me the opportunity to capture some amazing initiatives at his company. I can attest to Ryan's comment about their tours as I experienced the tour and it is extremely impressive and Remarkable.

Ryan's interview is a great example of how innovation and creativity can have a significant impact on a business.

What can you do in your business to disrupt how you deliver service to your customers?

_____

_____

_____

_____

_____

_____

# Becoming Best in Class

In 2012, I received a call from Stahl Peterbilt. They are an Edmonton, Alberta-based (with two other locations in Grand Prairie and Fort McMurray, Alberta) full service dealership that offers new and used medium and heavy duty truck Sales, Parts, Service, Finance, Rental and Leasing, and Body work. Stahl Peterbilt was looking to enhance their overall service levels within dealership branches and I was fortunate to gain their trust and support their business.

Stahl Peterbilt is still a valued customer and they do so many things remarkably well. They make it part of their mission to "consistently provide high-quality customer service in all areas of the business."

As a Best in Class dealership, they continually recruit and develop a customer-focused team.

Stahl Peterbilt provides a culture and environment of mutual trust and respect with all their employees, customers and suppliers. They also invest in their Best in Class facilities, which look highly professional and always pristine.

All team members and departments make it a daily focus to provide the best possible service to their customers. It has been a privilege to work with such a great company, filled with leaders who are constantly striving to make their business better, and for them, customer service is always top-of-mind.

*"The biggest thing I've seen in working with Mike Mack is the consistency right across the board to help support us as leaders, to develop the leaders that are working with us, to make the work place, the environment consistent right through all*

*departments, to ensure that we provide the best customer service possible."*
-Randy Kerr, Service Operations Manager

As I referenced earlier in my book, organizations that build Remarkable Service demonstrate value to their customers. This is an ongoing and constant focus for Stahl Peterbilt. It's part of their team DNA.

In addition, they leverage technology to obtain valuable feedback from their employees and customers so that they are constantly apprised of issues or concerns and they take corrective action to solve the problem quickly.

They have a cohesive team that constantly strives to service their customers. Stahl Peterbilt continuously provides their employees with coaching support, technical training, along with **soft-skill training**, that I have been privileged to support since 2012.

Stahl Peterbilt has recruited and supported great leaders over the years. The retention of their key team leaders is the envy of many organizations and they too, are open to learning, developing and receiving coaching support.

To validate this point, in early 2017, I launched The Five Behaviors of a Cohesive Team™Program (referenced earlier in the book) with the Senior Leaders of Stahl Peterbilt. This measures overall Trust, Conflict, Commitment, Accountability and Results as a collective management team. At the time of writing my book, Stahl Peterbilt had the highest ratings of any team or business that I have ever worked with. All scores are deemed best practice, which speaks further to Stahl Peterbilt's commitment to the process of improving their already great organization. The entire organization has been involved in training; from the receptionists, service technicians, outside part sales team, truck sales team, service advisors, to senior management, and with many receiving coaching support.

*"If you are looking to have a deep dive into your business and expand on your management team,*  *internal staff and are looking to bring your business to the next level and close more deals, you need to work with Mike Mack and his team. It's allowed us to open our eyes on how we work with each other on a daily basis and how we deal with customers, and as a team, we are all extremely satisfied with the progress."*
- Brent Lawrence, Parts Operations Manager

This is an excellent example of how a strong, successful business with a solid brand and excellent products still strives to continually improve and add value to their customers.

The list of countless awards that Stahl Peterbilt has received since acquiring the Peterbilt dealership in 2002 is Remarkable to say the least.

## 2017

Best in Class Dealer of the Year

Peterbilt Platinum Oval Winner, Edmonton

Peterbilt Platinum Oval Winner, Grande Prairie

## 2016

Best in Class Dealer of the Year

Peterbilt Platinum Oval Winner, Edmonton

Peterbilt Platinum Oval Winner, Grande Prairie

## 2015

Best in Class Dealer of the Year

Peterbilt Platinum Oval Winner, Edmonton

Peterbilt Platinum Oval Winner, Grande Prairie

## 2014

Best in Class Dealer of the Year

Peterbilt Platinum Oval Winner, Edmonton

Peterbilt Platinum Oval Winner, Grande Prairie

## 2012

Best in Class Dealer of the Year

Peterbilt Platinum Oval Winner, Edmonton

Peterbilt Platinum Oval Winner, Grande Prairie

## 2011

North American Best in Class Dealer of the Year

Best in Class Dealer of the Year

Peterbilt Platinum Oval Winner, Edmonton

Peterbilt Platinum Oval Winner, Grande Prairie

Parts & Service Dealer of the Year

## 2010

Best in Class Dealer of the Year

Peterbilt Platinum Oval Winner, Edmonton

Parts & Service Dealer o f the Year

Paccar Parts Winners Circle, Harold Properzi

Peterbilt Platinum Oval Winner, Grande Prairie

## 2009

Outstanding Service Management Excellence, Angelo Posteraro

Outstanding Service Management Excellence, Andre Doucet

## 2008

Best in Class Dealer of the Year

Peterbilt Platinum Oval Winner, Edmonton

Peterbilt Platinum Oval Winner, Grande Prairie

## 2007

North American Best in Class Dealer of the Year

Peterbilt Platinum Oval Winner, Edmonton

Outstanding Parts Sales Performance

## 2006

Best in Class Dealer of the Year

Peterbilt Platinum Oval Winner, Edmonton

Peterbilt Platinum Oval Winner, Grande Prairie

PacLease Standards of Excellence

Outstanding Service Management Excellence, Angelo Posteraro

Outstanding Parts Management Excellence

## 2005

Best in Class Dealer of the Year

Peterbilt Platinum Oval Winner, Edmonton

Peterbilt Platinum Oval Winner, Grande Prairie

PacLease Standards of Excellence

PacLease Northwest Region Award

PacLease Northwest Region Service Manager of the Year

Peterbilt Service Manager of the Year, Angelo Posteraro

Outstanding Parts Sales Excellence

Outstanding Service Management Excellence

## 2004

Peterbilt Platinum Oval Winner, Edmonton

Peterbilt Platinum Oval Winner, Grande Prairie

Medium Duty Dealer of the Year

Outstanding Parts Sales Excellence

## 2003

Outstanding Parts Sales Excellence

Their awards cabinet can no longer hold all the awards that they have received, simply because

it is packed full of plaques, trophies and recognition mementos.

Based on this extremely impressive list of awards and accolades you would think that Stahl Peterbilt might become complacent and believe that they are "great" and no further improvement is needed, but ironically, it is quite the opposite.

*"We have made a significant investment in our people and process improvements utilizing the services of Mike Mack and his team, with the objective of constantly improving overall Customer Service."*
-Eddy Stahl, President, Stahl Peterbilt Inc.

# What's Next?

First of all, a big thanks to you for taking the time to read my book. It has been a labour of love to write and revise the contents of this expanded edition.

It is my hope that you leave with valuable take-aways for your business. The reality is, there are tons of great ideas out there, whether it's in a book or on social media, but what is key to all of this, is ACTION and the EXECUTION of ideas.

Great people, leaders and business take great ideas and make them a reality. What's next for you?

List your top five next steps for your business:

1 _____

2 _____

3 _____

4 _____

5 _____

Do you think about Customer Service and more specifically, your Customer Service in a new light?

Delivering Remarkable Service is not impossible to achieve, but it will take effort and focus.

Take the time to determine what you are committed to improve upon and plan to focus your time and resources in that direction.

Meet with your team and review some of the questions that were listed in this book and get their input and thoughts.

Please don't hesitate to contact me, if I can be of any assistance to you and your business.

If you are ready, get started today as there is no time like the present to focus on improving your business. If you don't do it, your competitors will.

If you liked my book, I would be grateful for your feedback. You can visit either **amazon.com** or **amazon.ca**, search Mike Mack, *Remarkable Service - How to Keep Your Doors Open*, and post a review there.

Refer this book to your team, colleagues or business connections that may benefit from the key take-aways of this book.

Here's to your Remarkable Service Success!

*"What is the point of being alive, if you don't at least try to do something Remarkable?"*
-John Green, New York Times bestselling author

# Notes:

# Acknowledgements

I have many terrific and thoughtful business connections and friends in my world. As I made the decision to write this book in 2015 and create the revised edition in 2017, there were many great people and organizations involved in supporting me through the writing and creative process. In addition, I gained valuable insight over my career that allowed me new perspective and greater wisdom. They were all instrumental, and I want to thank each of them with my sincerest gratitude.

My amazing wife, Bonita Lehmann for always giving me unconditional love and encouraging me to *Dream Big*; Arnold McLaughlin...thanks for being such a dear friend, mentor and the best man at my wedding; Stahl Peterbilt Inc.; Strategic Coach and Shannon Waller, an amazing coach and guide; Shawna Soch...you were instrumental in making my book look so good and you must have read it 20 times before we sent it to the publisher; Gerry Lorente and Bavaria BMW; Matt Graff; Raymark Dizon; Michelle Clarke; Wayne Lee; Harvey Emas; Chad Griffiths...thanks for your push and friendship and for creating the amazing book cover; Stuart Bell, Betsey Vaughn and Kim Brandt from 90-Minute Books; Dave Carroll, Ron Tite; Jeff Tetz; Tim McClure; Tom Corley; Sawan Kapoor; Dr. Douglas Miller; Patricia Fripp; Ryan Vestby; Peter Kossowan; Lynn Cathcart of TEC Canada; Brent Lawrence;

Randy Kerr; James Morrissey and The Met Agency; Jeff Allen Productions; Joe Ammar, President of River City Events in Edmonton for being an amazing friend and community leader. You inspire me Joe; Rago Millwork and Supplies: Cucina Bella; Dennis Simpart; the late Vernon Hibbard; and my late parents, Tony and Helen Mack.

# Recommended Reading

*United Breaks Guitars: The Power of One Voice in the Age of Social Media* By: Dave Carroll

*Everyone's an Artist (or at Least They Should Be): How Creativity Gives you the Edge in Everything you Do* By: Ron Tite, Scott Kavanagh, and Christopher Novais

*Rich Habits: The Daily Success Habits of Wealthy Individuals: Find out How the Rich Get so Rich The secrets to Financial Success Revealed)* By: Thomas C. Corley

*The Culture Secret: How to Empower People and Companies No Matter what they sell.* By: Dr. David Vik

*The Five Dysfunctions of a Team: A Leadership Fable* By: Patrick Lencioni

*The Work of Leaders – How Vision, Alignment and Execution Will Change the Way you Lead* By: Julie Straw, Mark Scullard, Susie Kukkoken and Barry Davis

*The Healthy CEO: Taking the lead in your physical, relational and financial wellness* By: Dr. Larry Ohlhauser, M.D.

*Stop Talking...Get it Done!: The Leader's Guide to Bringing Vision and Action Together* By: Tyler Neilsen

# Comments about Remarkable Service

"*It's not enough to just talk about customer service, it needs to be constantly worked on. Mike's book helps you put tangible and actionable items to work to better increase your organization's customer service. He really packed this revised edition with great stories that will resonate with everyone." A great read on a crucial business topic.*" - Chad Griffiths, CCIM, MRICS Partner, Associate Broker NAI Commercial Real Estate Inc.

"*Business is so competitive today. Excelling at the basics is a start, but it's not enough. Customers expect and demand more! I have traveled the world over the course of my career, and there is one very valuable lesson that I've learned about customer service: It is the little things that make the biggest impact! Taking care of the small details separates one company from another, brings a level of satisfaction that is vivid and remarkable, and can ingrain a brand into the mind of the consumer for a very long time. Mike Mack capture's the essence of this message in his latest book. If you want to improve your bottom line, remember the importance of the small details. When that happens, you build a loyal customer base that will help you realize success well beyond the customer's initial experience with your brand.*" -Tim McClure, Professional Speaker, Brand & Leadership Consultant

*"The simplicity of Mike's message in his book Remarkable Service makes it a valuable read. It is my belief that every business in any industry can benefit from the insights that this book offers, and we must be reminded that the little things that are done consistently can make a big difference. At Arrow Engineering Inc. we strive to deliver Remarkable Service at every touch point of our customer's experience."* - Greg Burghardt, President & CEO Arrow Engineering

*"Remarkable Service is an easy read, but more importantly, providing Remarkable Customer Service is easier to achieve than many think. Mike Mack lays out a number of key strategies that any business can adopt, complete with great examples. You don't have to blow things up and start over to provide Remarkable Service – you can simply make incremental small changes that add up."*- Lorne M. Wight President & CEO, Allwest Commercial Furnishings

*"Customer Service is a vital component of our business regardless of the economy. Every member of our team is aware of the importance of going above and beyond to retain our valued customers. Mike Mack's book, Remarkable Service is a great reminder of what we must do during every customer interaction. When a customer has a challenge or problem, it must become our problem and we must make every attempt to solve the problem for our customer."* - Eddy Stahl President, Stahl Peterbilt Inc.

"*Mike Mack has an uncanny ability to create clarity about the key concepts of Remarkable Customer Service. His book provides simple, practical, plain language advice, using powerful and compelling anecdotes from real life, to put the delivery of Remarkable Customer Service within reach of all those who have the will to achieve it in their businesses. A great read.*" - Richard Morland, President, Northwest Territories Chamber of Commerce

# About The Author

Photo credits: Brent Lawrence,
**www.one2sixphotography.smugmug.com**

As an Entrepreneur, Business Advisor, Speaker, Facilitator, and Author, Mike has supported businesses since 2006.

He specializes in Customer Service, Sales, Team Building, Leadership Development, and Strategic Planning. It's Mike's belief that "Remarkable Customer Service" can lead to enhanced revenue and overall profitability. For Mike, it's about "trusted collaboration" with his customers. Mike holds an MBA from Athabasca University and is a proud member of Synergy Network (Edmonton Alberta Canada), serving as Chair in 2016; ACG (Association for Corporate Growth), President 2018-2019 for ACG Edmonton; Past member of Toastmasters International, obtaining his Distinguished Toastmasters Designation—DTM. The Distinguished Toastmaster award is the highest Toastmasters International bestows. The DTM recognizes a superior level of achievement in both communication and leadership; Member of CAPS (Canadian Association of Professional Speakers); TEC Canada Speaker; Past-President, Rotary Club of Edmonton Mayfield (2005/06). Mike and his wife Bonita live in Edmonton and love mountain biking in Edmonton's River Valley or in the majestic mountains of Alberta Canada. Mike's working on his next book: "RELATIONSHIPS FOR KEEPS" which is expected to be published in the summer of 2018.

# Connect with Mike Mack

Website:
**www.mikemack.ca**


Email:
mike@x5management.com

LinkedIn:
https://ca.linkedin.com/in/mikemackalberta

Twitter:
@x5mike

Instagram:
mikemackx5